II0666620

TOTALITARIANISM

EXPLORING WORLD GOVERNMENTS

ABDO
Publishing Company

TOTALITARIANISM

by Linda Cernak

Content Consultant
Jeremi Suri, E. Gordon Fox
Professor of History
University of Wisconsin
–Madison

CREDITS

Published by ABDO Publishing Company, 8000 West 78th Street, Edina, Minnesota 55439. Copyright © 2011 by Abdo Consulting Group, Inc. International copyrights reserved in all countries. No part of this book may be reproduced in any form without written permission from the publisher. The Essential Library™ is a trademark and logo of ABDO Publishing Company.

Printed in the United States of America,
North Mankato, Minnesota
112010
012011

♻ THIS BOOK CONTAINS AT LEAST 10% RECYCLED MATERIALS.

Editor: Melissa York
Copy Editor: Sarah Beckman
Interior Design and Production: Becky Daum
Cover Design: Becky Daum

Photo Credits: Shakh Aivazov/AP Images, cover, 3; Keystone-France/Getty, 9; Library of Congress, 16; AP Images, 21, 25, 45, 93, 101; Shutterstock, 33, 105; Harris & Ewing/Library of Congress, 55, 80; Pool/AP Images, 57; Johny Keny/Shutterstock, 64; Sarah-Jane Poole/AP Images, 71; APTN/AP Images, 77; Khin Maung Win/AP Images, 83; Javier Galeano/AP Images, 117; Fotolia, 123; Jeremy Edwards/iStockphoto, 127; Bobbly Earle/Fotolia, 131; Erin Lubin/AP Images, 137

Library of Congress Cataloging-in-Publication Data
Cernak, Linda, 1953-
  Totalitarianism / by Linda Cernak.
    p. cm. -- (Exploring world governments)
  Includes bibliographical references.
  ISBN 978-1-61714-795-1
  1. Totalitarianism. I. Title.
  JC480.C43 2011
  320.53--dc22
                                2010044461

Table of Contents

What Is Government?

In the earliest, simplest societies, government as we know it did not exist. Family or tribal elders made decisions, and their powers were limited. As civilizations grew, governments developed to organize societies and to protect them from outside threats. As societies have grown in complexity, so have the governments that organize them. In this way, organizing society has led to massive bureaucracies with many offices and roles.

As of 2010, there were more than 190 countries, each with its own government. Two governments may look very similar on paper even though political life inside those countries varies greatly. Every government is different because it is influenced by its country's history, culture, economics, geography, and even psychology.

Still, governments share some main roles. Today, a main function of governments is to protect citizens from outside threats. This has evolved into the vast arena of international relations, including military alliances and trade agreements. Governments also organize power in a society. However, how power is acquired—through elections, heredity, or force—varies, as does who exercises it—one person, a few, or many.

Ideally, governments balance the rights of individuals against the needs of the whole society. But who defines those needs? Is it leaders chosen by universal suffrage, or is it a single dictator who assumed power through force? How are individual rights protected? The answers to these questions distinguish one form of government from another.

Another role of government is preserving internal order—that is, order as defined by those in power. While keeping order might mean prosecuting violent criminals in a democracy, in a dictatorship, it could mean prosecuting dissenters. Governments also look out for the welfare of their citizens. All modern governments provide some form of social services, ranging from education to housing to health care.

Governments are often involved in their national economies. Involvement can run the full spectrum—from completely planning the economy to merely levying taxes and allowing a free market to operate. Governments also regulate the private lives of citizens—from issuing marriage licenses in a democracy to enforcing specific styles of dress in a theocracy.

While all governments have some characteristics in common, the world's governments take many forms and make decisions differently. How does a government decide what individual rights to give its citizens? How are laws enforced? What happens when laws are broken? The answers to such questions depend on the political system at hand. ⌘

1

What Is Totalitarianism?

It was June 1961 in France. One of the Soviet Union's most electrifying ballet dancers was performing with the Kirov Ballet in Paris. Rudolf Nureyev, who would go on to become one of the world's most celebrated dancers, went out and about in Paris despite strict orders from the Soviet government not to socialize with the French. The dance company boarded a plane for their next stop in London, England, but Nureyev was ordered to return home. Fearing he would never be able to leave the Soviet Union again, or worse, become imprisoned, Nureyev outwitted

Soviet dancer Rudolf Nureyev sought asylum while in Paris.

his KGB escorts, members of the Soviet secret police. He made a dramatic and daring dash for freedom at the airport and approached the French police to seek asylum, or safe haven.

More than two decades would pass after his defection from the Soviet Union before he was allowed to return to his homeland to see his dying mother.

Another story of attempted escape from a totalitarian regime took place in the Atlantic Ocean in November 1999. A small boat was navigating on the rough seas between Cuba and the United States amid 10-foot (3-m) high waves. A small group of people, including one young boy named Elian Gonzalez, had escaped their homeland of Cuba, risking their lives on a long journey across stormy seas. The boat encountered bad weather and sunk. Elian's mother died, but Elian was found clinging to an inner tube.

THE SOVIET UNION'S KGB

The primary intelligence agency in the Soviet Union from 1954 to 1991, the KGB, served as the "sword and the shield" of the Communist Party.[1] Although glamorized in many Cold War films and novels, such as Ian Fleming's *James Bond* series, the KGB was generally concerned with domestic security. At its peak, it was a fearsome and powerful intelligence organization, analogous to the United States Central Intelligence Agency. The KGB, however, spied upon the Soviet Union's own citizens, with its agents posing as businessmen or journalists. It used brutal interrogation practices to keep Soviet citizens in line and posted border guards to keep people from entering or leaving the country.

The young boy was taken to distant relatives in Florida, but ultimately returned to his father in Cuba.

On the opposite side of the world, US humanitarian Mike Kim defied six angry soldiers in Northern Laos in November 2004. The soldiers were pointing rifles at Kim, who had led two refugee women from North Korea through a 6,000-mile (9,700-km) underground railroad that ran through China and Southeast Asia. The women had hidden from border patrol soldiers, gone without food, and illegally crossed the border from China into Laos. They were only steps away from safety and freedom, but they were caught and taken into custody. The soldiers wanted to return the women to China, where they would be sent back to North Korea and most likely executed. Luckily, a large bribe and Kim's US passport convinced the soldiers to release them. Kim spent years in Korea, where he talked to citizens who trusted him with their stories. He helped many escape the country. In 2008, Mike Kim wrote a book called *Escaping North Korea* about his experiences helping North Korean refugees to safety. He did not mention the women by name to protect their identities.

These true stories took place on three different continents, but the people in them, a world famous dancer, a mother and her child, and two refugee women, all had something in common. What made them sacrifice everything to leave their homes and their possessions, knowing they may never return to see their families and loved ones? The countries from which these people escaped, the Soviet Union, Cuba, and North Korea, lacked the basic rights and freedoms of a democratic country, such as the United States. To varying degrees, each of these countries has exemplified a totalitarian government.

What Is Totalitarianism?

A totalitarian state is one in which the government controls almost all aspects of a citizen's life. When a totalitarian government gains control, existing laws, government systems, and traditions are replaced or destroyed. In a totalitarian state, citizens are told which political beliefs they should hold. The totalitarian state is driven by a system of beliefs, or central ideology, that is

ASPECTS OF TOTALITARIAN GOVERNMENTS

- Single-party government is controlled by a dictator or ruling regime
- Secret police employ terror tactics to control citizens
- Government controls the mass media through censorship and propaganda
- The government maintains central control of the economy
- Armies and weapons are controlled by the ruling regime
- A central ideology controls every aspect of citizens' lives

A totalitarian state is different from a dictatorship. A dictatorship might control a country's military or government, but does not dictate every aspect of a person's life, nor does it have a central ideology. An authoritarian state may use oppressive measures to control a population but does not control all aspects of its citizens' lives.

established by the ruling party. Everything the state does is to further the goals of that ideology. Citizens are forced, often through indoctrination, to conform to the ruling ideology. An ideology might be a political belief such as communism or fascism. Many totalitarian leaders also demand devotion or even worship from their subjects. The government tells citizens what jobs they must do, where they must live, and what they must think about government policies and leaders. Secret police spy on citizens, and there are few, if any, individual civil rights.

In a totalitarian system, there is an absence of democracy. Democracy is a system of government in which laws and leaders are decided by the consent of its citizens. A democracy generally has a written constitution guaranteeing individual rights, which are implemented by its laws. A totalitarian system offers little in the way of civil or individual rights. In fact, citizens are often subject to intimidation or forced into loyalty to the government or the dictator by spies, informants, and secret police. People who express dissatisfaction or disloyalty can be arrested and imprisoned without fair treatment or a fair trial. Leaders retain power by using tactics of unjustified arrests, torture, and execution.

In a totalitarian system, the government also controls most industries and businesses. A free market economy, in which business and industry is privately owned by citizens, is not generally allowed. Instead, totalitarian governments usually control their economies, planning the economy rather than allowing individuals to make their own economic choices. Labor unions, organizations of workers who strive to achieve common goals such as better working conditions, do not have independent power and are forbidden in some totalitarian states. Even religious practices and places of worship, if allowed at all by the government, are strictly controlled. The media is also controlled through censorship. The government owns most radio and television stations, and journalists do not have freedom to report on news that goes against the policies of the ruling power.

A totalitarian government is so invasive that it even controls theater, art, books, dance, and music. Works that speak out against the government are forbidden. Artists, musicians, and writers must create works that support the government and glorify it. Schools also serve the goals of the government, and teachers must adhere to lessons that support totalitarian policies. Even the books people

FREEDOM HOUSE

Freedom House is an independent organization that researches and advocates democracy and human rights throughout the world. Each year, the organization publishes an annual report that ranks countries around the world on their political rights, civil liberties, and state of democracy. The publication identifies the "worst of the worst" countries that violate human rights. In 2009, 193 countries and 16 territories were evaluated. Of those, 17 countries qualified as the world's most repressed societies, totaling 24 percent of the world's population.[2]

read are controlled, along with movies, television, radio, and the Internet. Everything a citizen reads or hears is censored by political power.

The Beginnings of Totalitarianism

Totalitarianism is a phenomenon of the twentieth century, with its beginnings rooted shortly after World War I (1914–1918). The first truly totalitarian state was the Soviet Union under the dictatorship of Joseph Stalin, who rose to power and took control in 1921. Stalin's Soviet Union was based on the political system of communism, the idea that equality in a society can happen only when there is no private ownership of property such as homes, farms, businesses, factories, or stores. Wealth is divided equally so there is no class system. In theory, a Communist state is not necessarily totalitarian; however, many Communist states past and present have been ruled by totalitarian leaders or regimes.

Benito Mussolini, dictator of Italy from 1922 to 1943, was the first person to use the term *totalitario* to describe his political goals. He believed that "everything is in the state and nothing human or spiritual exists, much less has value, outside the state."[3] Adolf Hitler succeeded in extending his totalitarian control over Nazi Germany to other countries, resulting in World War II (1939–1945). The governments of both Italy and Germany at the time were based on fascism, a political belief that regarded nationalism as more important than individual rights and

Stalin maintained totalitarian rule of the Soviet Union.

usually focused on the superiority of one group over another. Fascists practiced extreme, often violent policies.

Mao Zedong's China is another example of a totalitarian state that developed after World War II. In 1949, China underwent a Communist revolution. Mao rose to power, patterning the government after Stalin's Soviet Union. His totalitarian leadership was the direct cause of turmoil and economic disaster that would last well after his death in 1976.

Totalitarian Dictators

Some totalitarian states have been ruled by a group of leaders, such as a military junta or the leaders of a religion or a political party. However, the majority of totalitarian states have been led by dictators. A dictator is a person who rules with absolute power over a country or region. Dictators have ruled over countries, kingdoms, and territories for thousands of years. Not all dictators are totalitarian. Some are only concerned with personal power and wealth. Others exercise control over a government, usually with military force, without controlling every aspect of a citizen's life.

Dictators take control of a country in various ways. They may overtake an existing government through military force, or a coup d'état, such as the one that occurred in Burma in 1962, in which General U Ne Win took control. Some dictators, such as Hitler and Mussolini, are great orators. They give rousing, electrifying speeches that inspire a sense of nationalism and well-being, encouraging people and convincing them to give their undying support. A dictator may also install his or her own supporters in positions of power, so his or her policies will not be questioned or opposed. Or a dictator may inherit power, as in the case of Kim Jong Il, totalitarian leader of North Korea. A dictator may take control of a government that is already repressed with promises of more freedom or better conditions. Unfortunately, the new dictator may be even worse than the old regime. A dictator may even be a monarch, coming to power as the next member of a longstanding dynasty or ruling family.

Modern totalitarian dictators are able to use the media to strengthen their control. While it might have taken nineteenth-century French dictator Napoléon I several days to spread a message to his subjects over a long distance, it would take only minutes for twentieth-century dictators such as Hitler or Mussolini to get their messages to the public. With the aid of radio, film, loudspeakers, and other technologies, dictators can broadcast their message to entire nations, enforcing their will and governmental policies. Some modern totalitarian governments may even

THE WORST OF THE WORST 2009

Freedom House, an organization that advocates democracy and human rights, reports on the state of freedom in the world. Many of the 17 countries ranked as the world's most repressed societies are totalitarian regimes. The countries marked with asterisks are generally categorized as totalitarian states today. Others have aspects of totalitarianism.

- Belarus
- Burma (Myanmar) *
- Chad
- China
- Cuba *
- Equatorial Guinea
- Eritrea
- Laos
- Libya
- North Korea *
- Saudi Arabia
- Somalia
- Sudan
- Syria
- Turkmenistan
- Uzbekistan
- Zimbabwe *
- Chechnya (a disputed area controlled by Russia)
- South Ossetia (a disputed area controlled by Georgia)
- Tibet (a disputed area controlled by China)
- Western Sahara (controlled by Morocco)[4]

use surveillance, systems of observation through the use of cameras or other devices to spy on and keep track of citizens' activities. Surveillance is also used at borders to prevent people from leaving the country.

In the world today, there are many non-democratic countries. These authoritarian systems can take many forms, and some are closer to totalitarian systems than others. Many of these states keep tight control on some aspects of society but allow loosened control in others. Classifying states as totalitarian can also be controversial. Many experts argue about which aspects of a regime are totalitarian, or to what extent a country's government can be classified as totalitarian. ⌘

2

Fascism in Europe

Following the end of World War I in 1918, Europe was in a state of change as the empires of Germany, Austria-Hungary, and Russia broke apart. Monarchs lost their thrones, and Russia was immersed in a brutal revolution as Communists took control in 1921. The victorious nations of Great Britain and France faced massive debts. Economies were in chaos. More than 8.5 million people had died in the war. More than 20 million others had been wounded, and many would be handicapped for life.[1]

For millions of the soldiers returning home to countries devastated by war, life would never be the same. Houses, farms, businesses, factories,

The regimes of Hitler, left, and Mussolini, right, shared much in common.

and churches lay in ruins. Many of these soldiers were homeless; most were jobless. Refugees filled the streets, and unemployment was widespread. Rioting and fighting were commonplace. Famine threatened many regions. To add to the devastation of war, a worldwide epidemic of influenza swept the world in 1918, killing more than 40 million people.[2] The peace and prosperity the world had hoped for at the end of the war seemed a distant dream.

Beginnings of Fascism

All over Europe, men and women living in political, social, and economic chaos longed for leadership that would restore order and bring hope for a brighter future. The stage was set for two leaders to emerge. One, Benito Mussolini, would form a political movement in Italy called fascism. Its aim was to unite a country into a disciplined nation, under the rule of a single-party leader. Under the Fascist doctrine, Mussolini believed that having a strong nation was more important than the rights of individual citizens. He gained many followers with his dramatic speaking. Anyone who opposed those ideas would be violently put down by imprisonment, beatings, or other terror tactics. Another Fascist leader, Adolf Hitler, would bring the concept of a Fascist nation in Germany to a level that was unprecedented in world history by centralizing racism and anti-Semitism as part of his ideology. Both leaders gradually exercised their totalitarian control over two countries that were desperately in need of hope and security for citizens who had lost faith in their governments. However, the totalitarian regimes of these two brutal dictators would wreak havoc and destruction, culminating in World War II and the deaths of millions of innocent citizens.

Mussolini Rises to Power

Mussolini was the son of a blacksmith, born in 1883. In his earlier years, he was a Socialist, believing that all people should share a country's wealth equally, but his political views soon changed. In 1919, Mussolini organized a group into what would become the beginnings of the Fascist Party in Italy. He called the group *Fasci di Combattimento*, or "bands of fighters." The word *fascism* came from the Latin word *fasces*, which represented a bundle of sticks wrapped around an ax, a symbol of power in Roman times. Mussolini was a superb orator. His rousing speeches were dramatic and bold, inspiring ex-soldiers, students, and people opposed to Communist and Socialist views to form gangs. These Fascist squads, called the Blackshirts, began to spread throughout Italy, taking control of railroad stations, post offices, and public buildings. They rejected all other forms of government and used violence and terror tactics to oust local leaders. Many Italians did not fight back, as their faith in constitutional government had been lost.

In October 1922, Mussolini's Fascist groups declared a march on Rome, Italy. Fearing chaos, King Victor Emmanuel III appointed Mussolini as Italy's prime minister as a way to appease the Fascist leader. Several of Mussolini's Fascists held government posts, and as time passed, corruption spread throughout the government. Mussolini and his Fascists rigged elections and fought against other parties, sometimes using physical violence and terror tactics. They controlled the press and murdered or exiled those who stood in opposition. As Mussolini's power grew, he organized secret police to uphold the Fascist regime, now gaining strength in numbers. Italy's government, which in theory was a parliamentary monarchy, was now a Fascist police state, controlled by violence and terror. By 1925, Mussolini was in complete control. He took the title of *Il Duce*, "the Leader."

SONS OF THE WOLF

All boys in Italy were required at the age of six to join a youth society called the Sons of the Wolf. The group was described in a US War Department publication called the *Intelligence Bulletin* as a "Fascist incubator."[3] The purpose was to indoctrinate young boys to the Fascist movement from a very young age. Boys received military training in preparation for membership in the *Balilla* at the age of eight and eventually the *Avanguardisti* at the age of 14. All boys were required to join the Fascist Youth

at age 18. Mussolini's stated goal was to build a nation of warriors, bringing back the glory of the Roman Empire. However, the *Intelligence Bulletin* describes a different view of Mussolini's purpose:

While the boy is in the Balilla and the Avanguardisti, his training is directed by the Fascist Youth organization, which indoctrinates him with Party propaganda besides giving him preliminary military instruction.[4]

Italy under Fascist Rule

Although Mussolini became dictator of Italy, he did not abolish the monarchy or seek to destroy the Catholic Church. However, the Fascists became the sole political party. Mussolini exercised control over people in many ways. He allowed only state-controlled newspapers, and he abolished labor unions. In order to build a military, he encouraged growth in industries relating to military needs, such as metals and chemicals. Roads and railroads were improved to support military vehicles. A strong military also required a large population. Mussolini taxed single men in order to encourage them to marry. Married women were encouraged to have children and forbidden to work in government jobs. Youths were also encouraged to give their loyalty to Mussolini and the Fascist Party. At a very early age, boys were enrolled in youth groups that taught them military skills. Many people were required to swear loyalty to the Fascist Party in order to keep their jobs. Although Mussolini ruled as a Fascist dictator, his methods were not nearly as extreme as Adolf Hitler, who would go down in history as one of the world's most brutal dictators.

Adolf Hitler and the Rise of the Nazi Party

Like Mussolini, Hitler seized power through appointment by a ruling power. In January of 1933, he was appointed chancellor of Germany by German president Paul von Hindenburg. Hitler dreamed of uniting all German peoples and eventually conquering Europe. But perhaps the most chilling ambition was Hitler's desire to build a superior Aryan society by eliminating Jews, Slavs, and other groups he considered inferior. By the time he was chancellor, Hitler had already built a strong political party, the Nazi Party. The stock market crash of 1929 plunged the world into economic depression. The effects of this depression hit Germany hard. Unemployment was rampant, and a disheartened population longed for a leader who would bring them hope for the future.

Like Mussolini, Hitler was a brilliant orator, commanding attention and often whipping his audiences into a frenzy of adoration with his fiery speeches. His Nazi Party soon destroyed Germany's democratic republic government, and by 1934, Hitler had successfully eliminated his rivals within the party. Germany was now at the mercy of a single-party totalitarian dictator.

Germany under Nazi Rule

The Great Depression made life in Germany in the 1930s very difficult. At the beginning of the decade, the country faced terrible unemployment. Once Hitler came to power, people worked in factories building weapons and machines for Hitler's military and constructed new roads and buildings. However, labor unions were outlawed. Nazi loyalists were rewarded with homes, businesses, art, and belongings that had been taken away from Jews. Employment opportunities grew for Nazi loyalists as Jews and political opponents were pushed out of their jobs.

THE YELLOW STAR OF DAVID

Hitler set forth a policy in which every Jewish person was required to wear a yellow Star of David in public. If caught without it, the person would be beaten or imprisoned. Jews could also be punished if the star was not properly worn or displayed on the clothing.

All over Germany, the Nazi rule was evident. Once firmly in power, Hitler sought to control every aspect of a citizen's life. Loudspeakers were installed in schools, public buildings, and railroad stations so Hitler could address the nation with his messages at will. People were required to greet each other with the words, "Heil Hitler," by raising their right arm in a Nazi salute. German youths were required to belong to Nazi youth groups where they were indoctrinated into Hitler's ideals. Joseph Goebbels, Hitler's minister of Public Enlightenment and Propaganda, staged book burnings. Books written by Jews, Communists, or any other group perceived to be an enemy of the Nazi regime were burned in huge bonfires. The book burnings were celebrated with waving Nazi flags, marching bands, and soldiers.

Hitler believed in elitism, or rule by a superior class. He believed fair-skinned Aryans were superior because they were born that way. Those he considered inferior, such as Jews, Slavs, homosexuals, and gypsies, were not entitled to be part of Hitler's "master" race. People suffering from physical deformities and the mentally challenged were also included as

"Every child says 'Heil Hitler' from 50 to 150 times a day . . . The formula is required by law; if you meet a friend on the way to school, you say it; study periods are opened and closed with 'Heil Hitler!' 'Heil Hitler' says the postman, the streetcar conductor, the girl who sells you notebooks at the stationary store; and if your parents' first words when you come home to lunch are not 'Heil Hitler!' they have been guilty of a punishable offense."[5]

— *Erika Mann*, Facing History and Ourselves: Holocaust and Human Behavior part of this inferior group. Hitler believed his master race had a right to invade and rule other countries and crush Communists, Democrats, and Jews. His goals were clearly stated in his book *Mein Kampf* (*My Struggle*), written in 1925.

Hitler expanded Germany's borders by taking over Austria and parts of Czechoslovakia. He invaded Poland in 1939, sparking World War II. His war machine rolled over Europe, and soon his empire extended into France, Belgium, the Netherlands, Denmark, Norway, and parts of the Soviet Union. The Germans attempted to occupy England and parts of Africa. The defeat of Nazi Germany by Allied powers took several years, and it left in its wake millions dead, homeless, and displaced.

The Final Solution

Some Germans believed in Hitler's ideal of a superior race, and racism against Jews became commonplace. Perhaps one of the most horrifying examples of totalitarian dictatorship is evidenced by what happened in Germany under Hitler's regime. Hitler and his secret police, the Gestapo, systematically began to round up Jews, Communists, Slavs, gypsies, and other people considered undesirable. Nazi troops killed thousands of helpless victims and buried them in mass graves. The event is now known as the Holocaust.

In 1942, Hitler and his elite protection squad, a group of personal bodyguards known as the SS, began to implement their "Final Solution." They built large death camps, complete with a train system for transporting the victims. The people were put on huge trains like cattle and told they were being "relocated." In Hitler's Final Solution to the Jewish problem, more than 5 million people were exterminated. Many were gassed to death in huge gas chambers. The SS selected stronger people to work in the death camps, giving many of them the grim task of burying their own families and friends. The extent of this mass murder, or genocide, that took place was not fully known to the rest of the world until the Allies marched into Germany at the end of World War II. Sickened by the sight of the death camps and those few survivors, US and British soldiers documented what they saw so the world would never forget or repeat the horror of what happened in Hitler's Nazi Germany.

Rooted in a similar ideology of nationalism and ruling over societies geared toward military action, the totalitarian regimes in Italy and

THE GESTAPO

Perhaps the most feared of Hitler's Nazis were the members of the Gestapo, the Nazi secret police. They used brutal interrogation tactics and torture to round up Jews, Communists, and others considered a threat to the Nazi regime. The Gestapo operated outside the law, arresting people at will who were considered a threat to the German state. A person did not actually have to commit a crime to be imprisoned.

Germany had much in common. Both Mussolini and Hitler rose to power because their respective societies were desperate for leadership and stability amidst economic ruin. Radio and media played a key role in creating propaganda that surrounded the leaders, who were both charismatic and heavily militaristic. Understanding how totalitarian states such as Fascist Italy and Nazi Germany rose to power in the past can shed light on the actions of totalitarian dictators today. ⌘

3

Communism and Totalitarian Dictators

Few totalitarian dictators in history could equal the atrocious crimes of Adolf Hitler, but Joseph Stalin, who rose to power in the Soviet Union, and Mao Zedong, whose Communist Party took control of China, were brutal dictators whose actions also caused the death of millions. Although these leaders were Communists, with political policies that differed from the Fascist governments of Mussolini and Hitler, their totalitarian regimes ruled and regulated every

Chairman Mao's portrait hangs at Tiananmen Gate in Beijing, China.

请勿

aspect of life just as fiercely as their Fascist counterparts.

Stalin Rises to Power

When Vladimir Lenin seized power after the Russian Revolution in 1917, he created the world's first Communist state. Communism is a political and economic system in which the state controls all economic activities and owns all wealth. Communist states are not necessarily totalitarian, but under the dictatorship of Stalin, the Soviet Union became a totalitarian regime.

Stalin rose to power after the sudden death of Lenin in 1924. He engaged in a power struggle with a number of political leaders, but he came out on top, sometimes by murdering his rivals. As the general secretary of the Communist Party, he was able to use his influence to place his own supporters in important positions and turn party members against his opposition. He created an image of himself as a moderate leader who wished to simply follow in Lenin's footsteps. In reality, however, his ambition was to create a Socialist state in the Soviet Union that would result in a world revolution. Stalin believed that in order to create a strong Socialist state without the support of other countries, the Soviet Union would need to develop a strong industrial economy.

Stalin's Five-Year Plan

Stalin developed a Five-Year Plan with the main goal of increasing industry. His ideas were to put industry under government control and to collectivize farms. That is, all farms would be owned and controlled by the government and worked by a collective group of people. Under Stalin's plan, industry in the Soviet Union grew; however, most Soviet citizens could not choose their jobs. People were forced to give up their farms, move to the cities, and learn factory jobs. As a result, industrial production in steel, coal, oil, electricity, and motor vehicles grew steadily from 1928 to 1940. Working conditions for citizens were poor, however, and workers were encouraged to turn in coworkers who did not work hard enough. Private industry was not allowed. The government owned all businesses and made all economic decisions as to how resources would be distributed to the population. This was the opposite of a capitalist or a free market economy. A free market system encourages free enterprise, and its businesses are privately owned and run for profit.

PEASANT TREATMENT

While on assignment in the Soviet Union during the 1930s, American journalist Eugene Lyons described how Soviet peasants were treated:

A population . . . was stripped clean of all their belongings—not only their land and homes and cattle and tools, but often their last clothes and food . . . and driven out of their villages. They were herded with bayonets at railroad stations, packed indiscriminately into cattle cars . . . and dumped weeks later in the frozen North . . . there to live or die.[1]

Stalin also sought to establish a "classless" society by eliminating the wealthier peasants. Peasants were required to hand over all of their resources to the state-owned collective farms. Those who resisted were forcibly removed from their villages, imprisoned, or simply executed.

GULAGS

Gulags were forced labor camps in the Soviet Union, often located at the edges of brutally cold places such as Siberia. Surrounded by barbed wire fences, guarded by armed soldiers in tall towers, the prisoners lived in stark barracks that provided only the bare minimum requirements for life. Here, millions died from cold, labor, violence, and hunger. Anyone who spoke out against the government could be imprisoned. Peasants who kept food from collective farms to feed their families could be imprisoned. Even those who committed petty crimes could be sentenced to years of hard labor.

Farmers were not allowed to sell their surplus crops for profit, but instead had to hand them over to the government to feed industrial workers. As a result, many angry peasants rebelled and refused to grow grain. They also killed farm animals, destroyed tools and farm machinery, and burned existing crops. The result was devastating. Inadequate crop production in the Ukraine region led to widespread famine in 1932 and 1933. Six to seven million people died of starvation.[2]

Stalin's effort to eliminate agricultural capitalism and create a classless system among peasants resulted in millions more dead, exiled, and imprisoned. Wealthy peasants, the kulaks, were exiled to remote areas of the Soviet Union to forced labor camps called Gulags. Others were shot and killed. Ultimately, Stalin's goal of creating a classless system of people resulted in millions of deaths, but it tightened his control and gave him absolute power.

The Great Purge

Stalin's first Five-Year Plan succeeded in giving him supreme control, but he harbored fears that party members were plotting against him. In 1934, he began a reign of terror known as the Great Purge. Secret police targeted party members, industrial leaders, military officers, diplomats, writers, scientists, and ordinary citizens. The purge lasted for four years, resulting in millions executed, exiled to Gulags, or imprisoned. It is suspected that Stalin organized the murder of major rivals such as Sergei Kirov and Leon Trotsky, whom he believed to be his chief opposition.

Stalin sought to control religion and the arts as well. People could not practice their religions freely as he systematically destroyed churches and synagogues. Religious leaders were imprisoned or executed, and it was forbidden to teach religion in schools. There was no freedom of the press because the secret police used terror tactics against anyone who might speak out against the government. Propaganda denouncing democratic ideals and capitalism was everywhere. Musicians, artists, and writers were censored. All works of art were required to show life in the Soviet Union in a positive light.

The Beginnings of Communism in China

The people of China were similar to the peasants of Russia in that they had suffered under the rule of elite leaders. Absolute monarchs known as czars ruled Russia prior to 1917, and emperors had controlled the peasants of China for centuries. In both countries, people lived in poor conditions. Chinese peasants suffered from poverty and famine under the rule of the emperors. In 1911, Sun Yat-sen formed the Chinese Nationalist Party, or Kuomintang, a political party that wanted to do away with the imperial rulers of the Chinese dynasties. The Kuomintang supported a representative government and a strong national state. A series of revolts caused the last of the Chinese dynasties, the Qing Dynasty, to end. However, the first president, Yuan Shikai, was quickly taking dictatorial control. Away from the capital, local warlords controlled many of the provinces.

By 1920, Lenin's Communist Party had seized control of Russia, paving the way for the brutal regime of Joseph Stalin. During this same time period, a Communist state and another ruthless totalitarian leader emerged in China. In July 1921, a group of Chinese scholars met in Shanghai. They called for a revolution to take place and founded the Chinese Communist Party. One of those scholars was Mao Zedong, who would change the course of Chinese history.

During this time, no party or faction held control over the entire country or government, and several groups were jockeying for power. The leaders of the Communist Party in China believed the government should control the economy. However, the Chinese Nationalist Party argued for a representative government and a strong state. Mao spent his early years gathering together his Communist Party supporters. He believed China should be modernized in order to defend itself against foreigners. He felt that a strong army was necessary to implement his ideas for a Communist nation. He also believed the Communist Party would find support among the peasants. The promise of a better way of life through Communist ideals would set the stage for a revolution to take place.

> "A revolution is not a dinner party, or writing an essay, or painting a picture . . . A revolution is an insurrection, an act of violence by which one class overthrows another."[3]
>
> —*Mao Zedong*, Report on an Investigation of the Peasant Movement in Hunan.

In 1925, a young army officer named Jiang Jieshi became the leader of the Nationalist Party and began building a strong national military to defeat the warlords who controlled regional territories throughout China. His army quickly gained control over much of China. During this time, the Communist Party led a counterrevolution, leading workers and peasants in uprisings. In 1927, the Nationalist Party gained the upper hand, and the Communists fled into the mountains. Jiang wielded dictatorial power as he used the military to bring China back under his sole leadership.

The Communists began building military bases in remote areas, but were again chased back by the Nationalists between 1934 and 1936. At the time, Zhou Enlai led the Communist Party. Approximately 86,000 Communist troops retreated from the Nationalist army in what became known as the Long March. The march covered 6,000 miles (10,000 km) as the Communist troops trudged through mountain ranges and crossed rivers. Along the way, peasants joined the troops in support, forming the power base that ultimately enabled the Communists to take control. By the end of the march, Mao had taken control of the Communist Party.

The Rise of Mao's China

For much of World War II, the Communists and the Nationalists cooperated in order to fight against Japan. The conflict between the two parties was ready to break out again at the slightest provocation, however. The Nationalist Party lost power as the war continued and the government and the people ran out of money. It tried to maintain control by using secret police to stop dissidents. During the same time, the Communist Party was reenergized with new members.

Mao's Communist army, known as the People's Liberation Army, slowly gathered the support of the peasants, who felt that Jiang's leadership was corrupt and inefficient. They believed in Mao's promise of a better future based on Communist principles. Eventually, Mao's forces outnumbered and surrounded Jiang's Nationalist army, marching in Beijing and taking control of the capital. Jiang fled to Taiwan, vowing to return to China until his death in 1975.

Firmly in place as the leader of the Communist Party, Mao announced the birth of the People's Republic of China on October 1, 1949. Mao brought hope to a people who had suffered through a long civil war, hunger, poverty, and illiteracy. Mao, like Stalin before him, pledged to transform China into a modern industrialized nation, with goods, resources, and land fairly distributed among all people.

Mao's leadership led to a one-party totalitarian state, very similar to the one built by Stalin in the Soviet Union. His Communist Party ruled over everything and everyone. In 1953, Mao implemented the Five-Year Plan, based on Stalin's five-year plans for the Soviet Union. Under Mao, the government owned all industries and businesses. Land was redistributed among peasants and landlords in an attempt to reform the agricultural system. In order to accomplish this, Mao's Communists attacked and killed landlords who objected. Peasants began working on cooperative farms similar to the collectives of the Soviet Union. Industries developed, and railroads, canals, and hydroelectric plants were built. Iron, steel, and electric power increased. Little by little, Mao began to exercise even greater control over the lives of the people of China.

The Great Leap Forward

Mao's second Five-Year Plan, the Great Leap Forward, was established to increase agricultural output and industrialization. The government owned all land, and people were forced to give up their homes. People were required to live in large communes where everything was shared, eating in communal kitchens and living in dormitories. Communes were also organized to increase industrial development by building irrigation systems, dams, and steel furnaces.

> "Communism is not love. Communism is a hammer which we use to destroy our enemy."[6]
>
> —Mao Zedong

However, the Great Leap Forward proved to be a dismal failure. Inefficiency resulted in a lack of industrial and agricultural production. The government began to tax people in the form of grain, leaving little for people to eat. Although production was declining, the government believed that it was rising, so officials cracked down on starving peasants, accusing them of hoarding food. Between 1959 and 1961, at least 30 million Chinese people starved to death.[4] Some estimates rise as high as 45 million.[5] Yet Mao continued to praise his plan. As years went by, China recovered from the devastation of the Great Leap Forward, but the Chinese people continued to endure more suppression of personal freedoms under Mao's leadership.

Although Stalin, Mao, Mussolini, and Hitler ruled at different times and in different countries, as totalitarian dictators, they had many things in common. They all had an unbelievable desire for power, and their charisma enabled them to lead large groups of people, indoctrinating them with their ideologies. All four dictators resisted change and ruthlessly eliminated opposition, often with the use of violence. Their unbelievable rise to power was a combination of many factors. Dictators today employ many of the same techniques to attain power. ⌘

POL POT AND THE KHMER ROUGE MOVEMENT

Pol Pot, a brutal dictator who ruled Cambodia from 1975 to 1978, led the Khmer Rouge, a group of Cambodian Communists. They overtook the Cambodian government in 1975. Believing in an ideology of Cambodian nationalism, Pol Pot organized peasants to join the movement. He promised them a better life by eliminating capitalism. Under Pol Pot's totalitarian rule, he forced peasants to work on farms, ruthlessly killing any opposition. His economic policies failed, resulting in lost crops and economic disaster. Millions died of starvation or were executed. In 1978, Vietnam invaded Cambodia, and Pol Pot was forced into hiding. Although his Khmer Rouge allies were weakened, he continued his guerilla activities until he was captured in 1997 by opposing forces. Pol Pot died in 1998 of an apparent heart attack, although some suspect suicide or murder.

4

The Exchange of Power

It is difficult to imagine that three of history's most ruthless and inhumane totalitarian dictators, Hitler, Stalin, and Mao, were able to rise to power as popular leaders and maintain that power. The rise to power in a totalitarian regime can take place in different ways, depending on many different factors. A country that is prosperous and stable with a working constitution would not characteristically be vulnerable to a totalitarian government. Countries that suffer from poverty, economic

General U Ne Win, right, gained power in Burma through a coup d'état.

chaos, political corruption, or civil war are more likely to succumb to totalitarian rule.

Totalitarian leaders use a variety of methods to crush their opposition and control their supporters in their attempt to rise to power. Violence, propaganda, terror tactics, and manipulation are just a few ways totalitarian leaders are able to rule with absolute power. In some cases, leaders have faked elections by tampering with results or exerting pressure over voters in an effort to legitimize their rule.

Most totalitarian regimes are not stable and, thus, eventually fall and are replaced. Sometimes this happens with the death of the leader. In other cases, the regime ends violently in rebellion or war.

Gaining Control

Totalitarian dictators such as Hitler and Mussolini were genuinely popular at the start. Both men surrounded themselves with core supporters, eliminated opposing political parties, and established one-party systems. In Italy, Mussolini came to power legally by getting himself appointed prime minister. Hitler gained power by getting himself appointed chancellor by German president Hindenburg. In both cases, the appointments were made under times of duress in unstable governments. Once in power, these dictators suspended democratic government by exploiting economic and political instability to take totalitarian control.

Totalitarian leaders are able to increase their authority by surrounding themselves with supporters who will further their political and economic causes, as well as their quest for ultimate rule. They grant military and political appointments to those who support their policies and get rid of their opposition by various methods, including exile, imprisonment, and even murder. Some install relatives in positions of power. They may make promises of a better life to landowners, workers, trade unions, or religious leaders. Like Hitler, Mussolini, Stalin, and Mao, dictators often rise to power in countries that suffer from economic depression and political chaos. Promises of jobs, health care, education, and other reforms appeal to people who seek new leadership and hope for a better future. While some totalitarian leaders rise to power through the ranks of legitimate government, others take control through military force, often resulting in bloodshed, violence, and death.

The Coup d'État: Burma

The term *coup d'état* comes from the French word, *couper*, meaning "to cut." *État* means "state," so a coup d'état is literally a cut against the state. More precisely, it is a violent overthrow of the government. A coup d'état may be either a military victory or the overthrow of the government by a group or person that replaces the existing government. A military coup differs from a revolution in that a coup generally involves a much smaller group of people, whereas a revolution involves masses of people whose goal is social, economic, or political reform. Not all coups result in totalitarian states. A government can be controlled by the military, but the military powers may not control all aspects of a person's life. An example of a coup that resulted in a totalitarian state took place in Burma in 1962 and again in 1988.

After gaining its independence from Britain in 1948, Burma's government was formed as a democracy. The country, however, suffered from internal unrest. All of that changed on March 2, 1962, when General U Ne Win led a coup d'état. The army overthrew a government that had been elected by the people. He arrested Prime Minister U Nu and set up a ruling Revolutionary Council consisting of senior military officers. He abolished the constitution and with it the democratic government and civil rights. He set up a military government with Socialist economic policies, taking control of banks and businesses. Foreigners were ordered out of the country, and

COUP D'ÉTAT DICTATORS

Some current and recent examples of totalitarian leaders who took power through coup d'états:

- 1959—Fidel Castro leads the Cuban Revolution to overthrow dictator Fulgencio Batista but soon seizes power for himself
- 1969—Mu'ammar al-Gadhafi overthrows the monarchy in Libya
- 1979—Teodoro Obiang Nguema Mbasogo disposes and executes the leader of Equatorial Guinea, who happened to be his uncle

the government took over their businesses. Political mismanagement resulted in a repressed economy, impoverishing a once-wealthy nation.

General Ne Win's military regime ruled for the next 26 years, but prodemocracy demonstrations began to erupt in the 1980s as people became weary of years of repression and a severely depressed economy. It reached a horrifying climax in August 1988, when unarmed students led a demonstration calling for change. The demonstrators were attacked in a brutal military crackdown that killed an estimated 3,000 people.[1]

AUNG SAN SUU KYI

Aung San Suu Kyi helped organize the National League for Democracy in Burma. Fearing her popularity among the citizens of Burma, the military junta placed her under house arrest in 1989, where she remained on and off for years.[2] She was released on November 13, 2010. She was awarded the Nobel Peace Prize in 1991 for fighting in a nonviolent way against the military regime. Her collection of essays, *Freedom from Fear* notes, "It is not power that corrupts, but fear."[3]

The following September, a younger group of army generals staged another coup, replacing Ne Win's party. They established a ruling junta called the State Law and Order Restoration Council (SLORC). The military imposed martial law. The military served as the police and the legislature, and all civil rights were suspended. In 1990, the military junta allowed a multiparty election.

The National League for Democracy, an opposition group headed by Aung San Suu Kyi, won with an overwhelming majority. But the junta ignored the victory and placed Aung San Suu Kyi under house arrest. As of 2010, Burma remained a totalitarian state, persecuting individuals who oppose the military rule.

Inheritance of Dictatorships: North Korea

In traditional monarchies, the exchange of power occurs when an individual inherits power from a family member such as a king. Dictatorships are not usually inherited. However, when North Korea's totalitarian dictator Kim Il Sung died in 1994, his son and chosen successor, Kim Jong Il, became the country's new leader. Kim Il Sung had ruled North Korea for nearly half a century, from 1948 to 1994.

After World War II, Korea was divided into two parts—the Soviet Union controlled the north, exerting its Communist rule, and the United States backed the government of the south. Kim Il Sung had served in the Korean army during World War II. After the war, the Soviets considered him a hero for his part in fighting against the Japanese. The outside influence of the Soviet Union had a direct effect on Kim Il Sung's rise to power in 1948.

Kim Il Sung plunged his country into what became known as the Korean War. On June 25, 1950, he invaded South Korea in an attempt to unify both parts of Korea into one nation.

After the Korean War ended in 1953, Kim Il Sung tightened his control by purging his opposition and sending thousands of political prisoners to labor camps. He continued to rule North Korea in a Stalin-like dictatorship until passing his regime on to his son. Today, Kim Jong Il presents himself to the Korean people as their "Dear Leader." Loyal supporters surround him and dare not oppose his policies. He routinely spies on the citizens of North Korea and members of his own party through spy systems and secret police. Kim Jong Il ignores an economy in chaos and the hunger of his people. North Koreans are still suffering from the effects of famine in the 1990s, which killed more than one million people.[4] Instead, he spends government funds to increase the military. This includes the development of nuclear weapons despite international sanctions against them.

THE ETERNAL PRESIDENT

Several years after Kim Il Sung's death, he was declared the "Eternal President" of North Korea. As the Eternal President, hundreds of statues of Kim have been erected all over Korea, and his image appears in countless places all over the country.

How Dictatorships End

Totalitarian regimes can come to an end in a variety of ways, depending on a country's individual circumstances. War, intervention by other countries, internal rebellions against dictatorships, and military coups can depose even the most ruthless of dictators. World War II ended the regimes of Hitler, who shot himself to avoid capture, and Mussolini, who lost control of the government when his military plans went awry. Mussolini was caught trying to escape Italy in disguise. He was shot and his body was hung upside down in a public square.

Not all dictators come to such violent endings, however, and not all are deposed by wars. Stalin and Mao remained in power until their deaths in 1953 and 1976, respectively, and they retained their totalitarian control until the end. In the Soviet Union, Nikita Khrushchev replaced Stalin as dictator. He eventually lessened some of the tight control on personal freedom by launching a series of reforms that came to be known as de-Stalinization. Stalin's reign of terror was effectively ended, but Soviet citizens still suffered from a lack of civil liberties. Individuals desiring personal and artistic freedoms would continue to make daring defections to other countries, such as Rudolf Nureyev's famous escape in Paris in 1961.

Some totalitarian regimes have fallen to internal democratic movements as well. Eastern Europe in the 1980s saw a number of prodemocracy uprisings that helped the region shake off remaining aspects of Stalinism. One such example was the solidarity movement in Poland in the 1980s, led by Lech Walesa. Walesa formed a strong noncommunist trade union. After years of leading opposition workers against the

Communist government, the solidarity workers were able to hold elections and eventually formed a solidarity-led coalition government. Walesa was then elected president of Poland in 1990.

A totalitarian regime may even be ended by an invading country. This was the case when the United States invaded Iraq in 2003, removing Saddam Hussein from power. Invasion of a totalitarian state by a democratic superpower such as the United States does not ensure political stability, however. Fighting among different

SADDAM HUSSEIN'S IRAQ

Saddam Hussein reigned as Iraq's dictator until the US invasion in 2003. Hussein ruled over the single-party Baath government and made opposition parties illegal. Although Iraqis were encouraged to vote, they were subjected to terror tactics, arrest, torture, or execution if they did not support the Baath Party. Like other totalitarian regimes, criticism of Hussein and his policies was forbidden, and freedom of assembly was restricted to supporters of the Baath Party. Unlike Communist totalitarian regimes, which generally forbid religion, the state religion under Hussein was Islam. Shiite Muslims, however, were persecuted. Hussein's regime followed a policy known as Arabization, in which Kurds, Turkmens, and other non-Arab groups faced persecution, displacement, or mass execution. Hussein's mishandling of the government and economic sanctions imposed against Iraq because of its weapons policies created economic chaos in Iraq, leaving its citizens impoverished.

factions in Iraq continued despite efforts to establish democracy.

One Dictatorship Replaces Another: Cuba

A dictatorship can end as a result of a rebellion within a country. In Cuba, revolutionary leader Fidel Castro led a guerilla army against Fulgencio Batista in 1959. Batista was a brutal dictator who controlled the press and Cuba's congress. He embezzled funds from the country's economy and manipulated elections to ensure his continued control. Angered by the corruption and the repression of Batista's regime, Castro organized a group of revolutionaries to take control.

On January 1, 1959, Castro's revolutionary guerillas entered the capital of Havana. Batista, his family, and dozens of his government officials fled the country. Castro took control, executing the remaining Batista officials. Within two months, Castro became the prime minister of the revolutionary Communist government. At the time, Cubans looked toward Castro with great hope. But Castro merely replaced one totalitarian regime with another.

As of 2010, Fidel's younger brother, Raúl Castro, whom Castro placed into power in February 2008, ruled Cuba. Cuba remains a totalitarian dictatorship with a one-party system under the control of Raúl. Political dissent against the Communist Party of Cuba is illegal and punishable by imprisonment. Watch groups keep an eye on citizens who are opposed to the regime. News

Cuba's dictator Batista, center, was overthrown by future dictator Fidel Castro.

media and Internet access is under state control, and independent press is illegal. Journalists who work outside the government are subject to assault by state security agents or imprisonment. Most economic activities are controlled by the state. The government also restricts religious and academic freedoms as well as an individual's right to choose where to live or work.

The rise of a dictator is subject to many different factors. Not all dictators use force, and many are genuinely popular at the start. Economic factors play a huge role in the success of a dictator. If a dictator can capitalize on citizens struggling through harsh economic times, often that dictator can persuade the population to support the new regime and its ideology. ⌘

5

Cults of Personality, Propaganda, and the Secret Police

Rising to power to establish a totalitarian dictatorship is only the beginning. Dictators must also take measures to stay in power. In addition to surrounding themselves with supporters and crushing the opposition, some totalitarian leaders create cults of personality, supported by propaganda, secret police, and spy systems.

In North Korea, Kim Jong Il, right, maintains a strong cult of personality.

Cults of Personality

In his series of reforms known as de-Stalinization, Nikita Khrushchev was the first to coin the phrase "cult of personality." The idea originated with Karl Marx, the intellectual creator of communism, who discussed the concept of a "cult of the individual."[1] The cult of personality presents the leader as the savior of the people, of genius proportions and divine status. The leader is glorified and elevated to a level of adoration. Leaders are presented as intertwined with the state. They foster the belief that the state cannot survive without their rule. They believe their destiny is to rule their nation for eternity.

Successful totalitarian leaders generally build strong cults of personality by displaying their pictures everywhere on posters, billboards, and in public places. Followers put up statues, posters, and slogans everywhere. Speeches are reproduced in state-controlled newspapers and in books that fill up libraries and bookstores. The aim of the cult of personality is to make citizens believe in the absolute rule of the dictator and to justify even the most heinous of crimes and oppression. Citizens begin to feel as though the leader is everywhere. Cults of personality are driven by massive propaganda, with the aim of making the dictator seem benevolent, as well as all-powerful and indispensable to the future of the country he rules.

An outside observer might wonder what makes a person succumb to these tactics, or if the people living in the system really believe the propaganda. Natan Sharansky was a founder of the Adelson Institute for Strategic Studies at the Shalem Center in Jerusalem. He lived in a Soviet Gulag for nine years and formed an insight into how people respond to cults of personalities and totalitarian propaganda. As he explained, "Every totalitarian society consists of three groups: true believers, double-thinkers, and dissidents."[2] The revolutionaries and party members are the true believers, those who seek to uphold the power of the ruler. After a point, as the untruths and propaganda begin to unravel, these people become double-thinkers—people who live their lives as though they still believe but are beginning to doubt. Fear of violence or the secret police can keep people from taking action. When people can no longer pretend, they become dissidents and begin to actively fight against the ruling regime. According to Sharansky, in each totalitarian society, people progress through these stages at different rates until dissidents hit a tipping point and rebellion occurs.

Masters of the Personality Cult

Stalin, Hitler, Mao, and Kim Il Sung and Kim Jong Il, among others, were masters of creating a personality cult. Stalin has been credited with establishing the first of the twentieth-century personality cults. He linked himself to Lenin, who established the Communist Party in the Soviet Union. Lenin was glorified after his death, and Stalin capitalized on that glorification by associating himself with Lenin's accomplishments. One tactic he used was to rewrite history. He pretended he had been Lenin's chief adviser in

1917, when in truth he had been a newspaper editor. Press coverage of Stalin's fiftieth birthday described him as "a beloved leader, the truest pupil and comrade-in-arms of Vladimir Illich Lenin."[3] Despite the many deaths Stalin caused, many Russians still consider Stalin a great leader and national hero.

Hitler and Mussolini were also masters at creating cults of personality around themselves. Both held massive rallies to impress their audiences with their policies and to play upon people's emotions. Mussolini's punctuated gestures and staccato speeches could whip crowds into a frenzy of admiration for their leader. Hitler practiced his speeches in front of a mirror, crafting his voice and his gestures to give the effect he desired. Bands, banners, and flags accompanied his speeches, while brightly lit torches and floodlights focused only on him so listeners would not be distracted. Like other dictators who created a cult of personality, their faces and slogans were everywhere on posters, on billboards, and in public places. The spectacle of Hitler's goose-stepping Nazis added to his personality cult as an all-powerful leader who would restore Germany to its former greatness.

In more recent times, Saparmurat Niyazov, dictator of Turkmenistan until 2006, and Kim Jong Il of North Korea have formed notable personality cults. In Turkmenistan, which gained independence from the former Soviet Union after its collapse, Niyazov become the new republic's first president in an unopposed election in 1991. He began creating a cult of personality at a very high financial cost to the citizens of Turkmenistan. Niyazov nicknamed himself "Head of the Turkmen," and he put his picture everywhere, including the country's currency. He renamed streets and city buildings after himself. Generously including his family in his personality cult, he renamed the days of the week, months of the year, and a crater on the moon in their honor. He used his nation's funds to build projects that promoted his prestige, including a golden statue of himself that sits on top of a 246-foot (75-m) marble monument called the Neutrality Arch.[4] The statue was designed to rotate, continually following the path of the sun.

In North Korea, Kim Jong Il continues his father's cult of personality by erecting thousands of statues in his likeness all over the country. One statue of Kim Il Sung sits in the capital city of

CULT OF PERSONALITY AND KIM JONG IL

Korean journalist Kongdan Oh, a scholar who coauthored the book, *North Korea through the Looking Glass*, described Kim Jong Il in the following passages:

> By all accounts, the Dear Leader's favorite task was running the state propaganda machine, which he gleefully used to deify his father—and by extension, himself. Today his picture hangs next to his father's in every building.[5]

> It's a cult of personality like nothing in history. In North Korea he and his father are like God and Jesus Christ.[6]

Pyongyang. It is more than 75 feet (23 m) tall. In addition, Kim Jong II has installed dozens of mosaic images of himself and his father all over the country. In 2008, at least 88 murals were constructed.[7] Kim also made it mandatory that every household own a picture of him, and walls of schools, libraries, and public buildings are covered with his image. People are even required to wear a badge with his picture on their clothes. It is intended to be a symbol of national pride.

Propaganda in Totalitarian Dictatorships

In general, propaganda is information that is intended to manipulate the public into thinking or believing something. Hitler wrote in *Mein Kampf* that people "more easily fall a victim to a big lie than to a little one."[8] The use of modern communications such as radio and television have enabled dictators to exert more control over their citizens through such lies. In some totalitarian regimes, such as North Korea, propaganda about the greatness of a country's particular leader blares from state-controlled radios and televisions. Hitler even had loudspeakers installed in public buildings and schools so he could address the nation at will. In many countries, newspapers are highly censored so dictators can keep events they do not want the public to know about secret.

Propaganda films and newsreels are designed to glorify the ideology and leaders of a particular regime and to present distorted views of democratic countries. In fact, one of the most famous propaganda films was made in the Soviet Union under Stalin. The film, called *Our March*, was released in 1968 to celebrate the fiftieth anniversary of the Communist takeover of Russia. The film glorifies Lenin and the 1917 revolution but ignores and distorts the problems that existed at the time. It also depicts opposition to the Communist regime as wicked and cruel.

Slogans are another method of propaganda designed to reinforce a totalitarian dictator's ideology. For example, one Soviet poster showed a group of construction workers with the slogan, "Building a Communist Paradise." In China, a slogan reads, "Serve the People." During the 1990s, in an effort to slow population growth, the Chinese government spread the slogan, "It is good to have just one child." In North Korea, a

BIG BROTHER IS WATCHING

British author George Orwell wrote *1984*, his chilling novel about a totalitarian society, after the end of World War II. The world was just becoming aware of the true horrors of Stalinist Russia and Nazi Germany. In his novel, Orwell describes a world made up of three empires at war. The war is actually a lie, but people are made to believe that it is real. This allows the Party, otherwise known as Big Brother, to justify its actions. Terror tactics and the Thought Police intimidate citizens, and homes have telescreens that allow the government to spy on them. The main character of the book fights against the Party, but in the end, propaganda and torture make this character believe he actually loves Big Brother.

*Propaganda is an effective tool
used by dictators.*

slogan calls for people to remember "Let's devote
our lives for Kim Il Sung," on the celebration
of his sixtieth birthday.[9] By introducing slogans
into the daily lives of citizens, dictators provide
principles for people to live by. The slogans are
intended to replace religious prayers or other

traditional sayings that do not support the ruling ideology of the government. Even salutes are a type of slogan. The Nazi salute "Heil Hitler" replaced "Good morning" and other typical greetings. Even children were required to begin their day with a "Heil Hitler" salute.

Propaganda also finds its way into school systems. Indoctrination in a totalitarian state's particular ideology begins at an early age. School children are taught about the great deeds of the country's leader. Education systems do not encourage creative or independent thinking. Instead, rote learning controls what students think. Students are required to join youth organizations that further mold their thinking.

In Nazi Germany, boys and girls joined the Hitler Youth and swore allegiance to Hitler. In Italy, youth organizations such as the Sons of the Wolf trained young boys in military tactics. Today, a youth organization called the Young Pioneers has members in Communist countries such as Cuba, Vietnam, and China. The Young Pioneers teaches boys and girls up to the age of 13 about communism. It conducts civic activities as well, such as parades and volunteer work. In China, boys and girls go on to join the Communist Youth League, which teaches political education and military training.

Spies and Secret Police

Totalitarian dictators retain their power by creating a police state, a country in which the government asserts its power through a vast network of secret police, spies, and military forces. Many of these groups operate outside the law, using terror tactics, torture, intimidation, and spying to force citizens to obey the rules of the regime. In many cases, arrests are made without warrants, and prisoners can be held for an indefinite period of time. Secret police use informants to spy on ordinary citizens who are suspected of opposing the government. Citizens must be careful of what they say, never knowing if a listener, perhaps even a family member, is working as a spy for the government. Suspects can be tortured into making false confessions and providing names of innocent people who are subject to further terror tactics. Secret police also arrest or detain foreign visitors for suspected opposition activity. People who oppose a regime can also be apprehended and forced to live in camps where they are "reeducated" or

COMMUNIST YOUTH LEAGUE

The Chinese Constitution contains information regarding the purpose of the Communist Youth League of China:

Chapter X, Article 50: Party committees at all levels must strengthen their leadership over the Communist Youth League organizations and pay attention to selecting and training League cadres [activists]. The Party must firmly support the Communist Youth League in the lively and creative performance of its work to suit the characteristics and needs of young people, and give full play to the League's role as . . . a bridge linking the Party with great numbers of young people.[10]

indoctrinated with the ideology of the ruling regime. The rules then become internalized until they become a way of life.

Perhaps the most infamous of the secret police services were Hitler's SS and the Soviet Union's KGB. Hitler's SS was a group of his personal bodyguards. On June 29, 1934, he used his SS bodyguards to murder members of the SA (the Nazi Party's militia) and others who were believed to be political opponents of Hitler. Hitler worried he had lost control over the SA. The incident later became known as the Night of the Long Knives. Hitler presented propaganda to the German people about a fake SA plot against the government to justify his actions. The world was shocked at the murders. Many of the German

THE KGB 1967 ANNUAL REPORT

The annual report of the KGB of 1967, delivered to Premier Leonid Brezhnev in 1968, gave an account of activities of some 167,000 agents in the Soviet Union. The report contained information about the arrest of 34 suspected spies, the arrest of 1,200 people for writing or printing material critical of the Soviet regime, and the confiscation of such literature. The report also included information about 221 people who were trying to leave the country without permission and 6,747 people who were being followed and spied upon with listening devices in their homes or telephones. More than 12,000 people were interrogated by the KGB and warned with threats of arrest and possible torture if they took part in anticommunist behavior.[11]

people, however, believed the propaganda, commending Hitler for his actions.

Today, some states that have secret police organizations include Belarus, North Korea, the Russian Federation, Turkmenistan, and Zimbabwe. In North Korea, dictator Kim Jong Il appointed his third son, Kim Jong Un, as chief of intelligence of its secret police organization, the State Security Department, in 2009. By 2010, Kim Jong Un was poised to succeed his father as the next dictator of North Korea. In the Russian Federation, the Federal Security Service (FSB) replaced the notorious KGB after the collapse of the Soviet Union in 1991. The FSB is mostly involved in domestic fights against organized crime and terrorism. Turkmenistan's secret police agency has been reported to terrorize religious

RUSSIA SINCE THE COLLAPSE OF THE SOVIET UNION

In 1991, after the dissolution of the Soviet Union, the Russian Federation became an independent state led by Boris Yeltsin, the elected president. The new Russia was vastly different from the totalitarian dictatorship of the Stalin era. Elections were held under a multiple-party system, and the state moved toward democratic and economic reforms. The road to democracy has been difficult, however. The citizens of Russia are still subject to some police terror tactics, and the current government has moved back toward tighter control of the media, religion, and academics. Although Russia is now a multiparty state, corruption among government officials will challenge the people of Russia to continue to move toward democracy.

groups, which are strictly controlled by the government.

Spreading propaganda, using secret police and spies, and creating a cult of personality are all techniques that dictators use to take power and to maintain that power. They use the media to reach widespread audiences, making the use of these techniques unique to the modern age of technology. Once in power, these dictators use other methods to exert totalitarian rule over citizens. ⌘

6

The Right to Vote

Many totalitarian states have constitutions that guarantee citizens the right to vote and elect their leaders, but in reality, these rights are not practiced. In the United States and other democracies, citizens vote on candidates to fill government offices. Measures are taken to verify accurate vote counts and ensure that every qualified citizen has the opportunity to exercise this right. Many democracies have two-party systems that present a platform of their policies. Some countries use a voting system of proportional representation. That means that the seats in the government are awarded in proportion to the amount of votes counted.

Zimbabwe's President Mugabe voted in a 1996 election he was assured to win due to opposition withdrawals.

For example, if a party receives 35 percent of the votes, then that party is allowed 35 percent of representation in its government.

Totalitarian governments do not allow their citizens the right to elect their leaders in a democratic manner. Elections may not be held at all, even if they are guaranteed in a country's constitution. There are no term limits placed on totalitarian dictators since it is the dictators who make all of the policies. For example, Fidel Castro served as dictator of Cuba for 49 years, Kim Il Sung ruled over North Korea for 50 years, and Mu'ammar al-Gadhafi has ruled Libya since 1969.

Many elections that do take place in totalitarian regimes are rigged. Voting results are faked or tampered with to ensure the leader stays in power. Elections are staged to give an appearance of democracy to citizens. Secret police and

ELECTIONS IN CUBA

In Cuba, the elections are not considered free or fair. That country's constitution allows for elections, but the elections do not reflect the ideals of an electoral democracy. The National Assembly of People's Power and its Council of State make up the legislative branch of the Communist government of Cuba. However, in the January 2008 elections, all of the candidates for the National Assembly had to be pre-approved by the Communist Party (CP). As a result, the CP won 98.7 percent of the votes. The "election" allowed for 607 of the 614 seats in the National Assembly to be members of the CP.[1]

supporters of the regime often intimidate and threaten citizens to vote for the ruling party. Journalists who report on political parties in opposition to the ruling dictator or party are often subject to arrests, beatings, and harassment. Such is the case in Zimbabwe in elections that have taken place over the past decade.

Disputed Election Results

Robert Mugabe was elected prime minister of the newly independent Zimbabwe in 1980. This put his party, the Zimbabwe African National Union-Patriot Front (ZANU-PF), in control of the government. Over the years, Mugabe became increasingly authoritarian as a leader. The government became more corrupt, and fraud became more and more apparent in subsequent elections.

Amendments made to the constitution gave Mugabe even more authority over the executive and legislative branches. This, and increasing economic trouble, led to an opposition to the ZANU-PF party in the form of the Movement for Democratic Change (MDC), led by Morgan Tsvangirai. The MDC is made of trade unions and other civil society groups.

In the 2002 presidential election, Mugabe influenced voters by using violence and other intimidation tactics against MDC opposition supporters. Mugabe won the election by 56 percent to 42 percent over candidate Tsvangirai, but reports surfaced of an election rigged through violence, intimidation, and bribery.[2]

The MDC contested the results, claiming the election process was flawed. Only ZANU-PF members were allowed to monitor polls and election procedures. Displays of campaign posters and election fliers were restricted for the MDC.

The following year, intimidation and terror tactics continued against MDC supporters during the parliamentary elections. Aspects of totalitarianism became more and more apparent as the government passed legislation that restricted civil liberties such as free speech, freedom of the press, and the right to assembly.

TERROR TACTICS IN ZIMBABWE

A newspaper in the United Kingdom, the *Guardian*, reported on the 2008 elections in Zimbabwe. The opposition party, Movement for Democratic Change (MDC), initially appeared to defeat the sitting president, Robert Mugabe. The MDC had not expected to win. The electoral commission had not yet certified the official results when a group of armed men came to arrest the MDC leader. Sandati Kuratidzi, a party activist, explained:

> They warned people that if they voted for the opposition they would be killed. They had AK-47s, shotguns, guns in their belts. People were very afraid. . . . They were saying they were going to show an example to anyone supporting MDC and they asked the people to point out who they were but no one did. Their behavior was inhuman.[3]

In 2005, the government began a program known as Operation Restore Order. Program officials searched urban areas under the pretext of ridding the areas of illegal businesses and criminal activities. As a result, about 700,000 people were forcibly removed from their homes and lost their businesses.[4] Government police destroyed homes and businesses, and thousands were left without food and shelter. The people targeted in this massive operation were those who had supported Tsvangirai and the opposition MDC. The government even threatened voters by holding back food resources from potential MDC supporters.

In the 2008 elections, Tsvangirai defeated Mugabe's ZANU-PF party with 47.9 percent of the vote as opposed to 43.2 percent for Mugabe. A third-party member received 8.3 percent.[5] The release of the election results was delayed, and the government declared a runoff election would be necessary because neither candidate received a majority vote. Once again, the ZANU-PF party began its terror tactics against the MDC supporters. Hundreds of innocent MDC supporters were killed in government-supported violence. Tsvangirai claimed that fair elections were not possible. Fearing more violence against his supporters, he decided not to contest the runoff vote or boycott Mugabe's uncontested victory. However, as a result of domestic and international protests against the ZANU-PF government, an agreement following Mugabe's presidential inauguration in 2008 made Tsvangirai prime minister.

Election Results Ignored: Burma

In some countries, elections take place and the ruling dictator is defeated, but the ruling party will still stand in the way of the newly elected government or party leader. Leaders who are rightfully elected are often not allowed to take control of a country. Totalitarian dictators and governments find ways to make the elections invalid. Such was the case in Burma in 1990.

A military junta known as the State Law and Order Restoration Council (SLORC) took power in a military coup in 1988. In 1997, the military junta renamed itself the State Peace and Development Council (SPDC) and currently runs the Burmese government with the same totalitarian control. However, in 1990, the first free election in over 30 years took place in Burma, in response to increased international scrutiny after the 1988

ZIMBABWE: ASPECTS OF TOTALITARIANISM

Zimbabwe has many aspects of a totalitarian regime in spite of the efforts of opposition leader Morgan Tsvangirai against the Mugabe regime. In Zimbabwe, the state controls newspapers, broadcasting, and all other media. Schools are under state control with little, if any, academic freedoms. Travel, residence, and property rights are severely restricted by the government, which has evicted citizens and landowners at will. Civil rights are ignored as state police subject citizens to searches, seizures, and torture tactics. Although religious freedoms are allowed, many churches support the dictatorship of the Mugabe regime.

Aung San Suu Kyi had been imprisoned for supporting democracy in Burma.

coup. The military junta assumed that their party would win because voters would be intimidated to vote otherwise. Opposition party leader Aung San Suu Kyi formed the National League for Democracy (NLD). She won the election in a landslide victory even though she had been under house arrest since 1989. The NLD won an overwhelming 392 seats of the 485 seats in Burma's parliament.[6] In order to keep control, the SPDC refused to acknowledge the election results, and Aung was not allowed to take power. The SPDC also refused to allow parliament into session with its newly elected NLD party members. The military government also responded by imprisoning many members of the NLD.

BURMESE ELECTION LAWS

The new 2010 election laws in Burma have garnered criticism from around the world because they do not allow key members of the National League for Democracy to run for office. Explained Philippine Foreign Secretary Alberto Romulo, "Unless they release Aung San Suu Kyi and allow her and her party to participate in elections, it's a complete farce and therefore contrary to their roadmap to democracy."[7] Argued US State Department spokesman Philip Crowley, "The laws made a mockery of the democratic process and ensures the upcoming election will be devoid of credibility."[8]

Since the 1990 election, Aung and her NLD party have continued their efforts to oppose the military regime in Burma. The SPDC kept Aung in and out of house arrest or prison for a total of 15 years out of the past three decades. However, in 2002, Aung was allowed to leave her home, and she continued to travel the country and gather support for the NLD. In 2003, while traveling with a large group of NLD members, supporters of the military regime attacked her group. Some NLD members were killed and others were injured. Some fled, fearing further assault. Aung was released on November 13, 2010.

Over the years, the NLD, Aung, and her supporters have continued to fight for democratic principles in Burma. However, these protestors are subject to arrest and imprisonment. Today, the military junta still maintains its tight control over the people of Burma. In 2010, the government declared the results of the 1990 election invalid. Government officials claimed the election had taken place under a law that had since been revoked by new legislation. In addition, the military regime has formed new laws that prohibit people with "criminal records" from belonging to or forming political parties. This effectively bans Aung and other party members who have been imprisoned from running for office. The bans ensure that the military has control over the NLD and Aung. The battle for democracy and free elections continues today in Burma. In fact, the ruling military junta has taken steps to revise its constitution, giving their regime even more power.

Electoral Democracies

The United States and many other democratic countries are said to have electoral democracies. That means that people choose their leaders by casting votes, and those leaders form a ruling body that makes decisions for the people. But that is only part of democracy. The governing body, such as a congress or a parliament, must make decisions based on the protection of civil liberties and the rule of law. That is, governance must protect the rights of citizens. Government authority may only be exercised according to written laws such as those stated in a constitution.

*The United States has a long tradition
of free and fair elections.*

Burma and Zimbabwe are not electoral democracies because their leaders, a military junta and a dictator, rule by decree. The ruling bodies control all levels of government with no system of checks and balances—the executive branch, the legislative branches, and the judiciary branch. Without a system of checks and balances, these ruling powers impose laws at will, overriding existing laws and old written constitutions. In Burma, the ruling military holds government positions. In Zimbabwe, Mugabe and the ZANU-PF party have made changes to the constitution that give them more power. In both places, people who oppose the government are often imprisoned, intimidated, or threatened. Some even lose their lives.

The right to free and fair elections is a key civil liberty in democratic governments. But in totalitarian governments, elections are either forbidden or the only party that citizens can vote for is the ruling party. By outlawing other political parties, using intimidation tactics, and manipulating election results, the denial of this basic civil right is another way that totalitarian regimes maintain power. ⌘

7

Human Rights

Many totalitarian governments have constitutions that guarantee civil liberties, such as the right to vote, freedom of speech, freedom of the press, the right to assembly, the right to a fair and speedy trial, and the right to follow the religion of one's choice. However, the governments do not uphold these civil liberties for citizens. Some totalitarian states do not have a constitution. Others have rulers such as dictators or military regimes that make changes to their constitutions at will, giving and taking power to their advantage. Forbidding rights such as freedom of speech and freedom of the

Citizens of Burma read state-run newspapers.

press enables totalitarian regimes to control the actions of citizens who publicly oppose their leadership.

Although some totalitarian states have branches of government (executive, legislative, and judicial), power and control lie solely with the ruling dictator or group. Or in some cases, ruling party members control all the branches of government, so there is no system of checks and balances.

Freedom of the Press

Most totalitarian regimes do not allow free or independent media, including the Internet, newspapers, magazines, radio, and television. By controlling the information that people are allowed to receive, totalitarian regimes can maintain support and suppress opposition. Regimes use the press and other forms of media to create propaganda that shapes people's opinions and ideas about their government and events. State-controlled news agencies print newspapers and control what is broadcast over radio and television. The Internet is also strictly controlled. In some cases, the cost of an Internet connection is so high that the average citizen cannot afford it. Some regimes censor search results or restrict the Web sites citizens can visit. In addition, journalists risk imprisonment, threats, and acts of violence against them if they report news events or write editorial opinions that are critical of the ruling regime. Foreign newspapers are banned to prevent citizens from reading about democratic countries and opportunities in other parts of the world.

In 2009, the Freedom House report *Freedom of the Press 2010* rated these countries as the ten worst countries in press freedom: North Korea, Turkmenistan, Burma, Libya, Eritrea, Cuba, Uzbekistan, Belarus, Equatorial Guinea, and Iran. In fact, 32 percent of the countries surveyed were determined to not have free press.[1] Although some countries have constitutions that allow free press, the freedom is not practiced. For example, Turkmenistan has a constitution that allows for freedom of the press, but the ruling government allows only state-controlled radio and television. Libya, which has no working constitution, also has state-controlled radio and television. In Cuba, the Communist Party controls the news media. The independent press is illegal, and government agents spy on news agencies that are suspected of reporting on news events outside of the government control. Journalists and their families are subject to harassment.

FREEDOM OF THE PRESS INDEX

The *Freedom of the Press* index is an annual survey of global media freedom that evaluates the level of print, broadcast, and Internet freedom in all countries of the world. Countries are ranked on a scale of 1 to 100. The index studies factors such as the political censorship, the ability of media reporters to cover news events, the use of violence and intimidation against reporters, and media ownership.

Totalitarian countries such as North Korea and Burma have all of the radios and televisions fixed to state channels so the government can report their version of news events. In Burma, the constitution allows for freedom of speech and freedom of the press. However, the 1962 Printers and Publishers Registration Act censors news content by requiring journalists to have what they write approved by government authorities. Violators are subject to arrest and imprisonment. In 2008, a number of prominent journalists were arrested for violating the Printers and Publishers Registration Act by expressing their political views. The editor and the office manager of *Myanmar Nation* magazine both were sentenced to seven years in prison. Prior to the 1962 military coup in Burma, there were at least 39 newspapers published in a variety of languages, including Burmese, English, and Chinese. One by one, the newspapers closed down as the government

LIBYA: ASPECTS OF TOTALITARIANISM

In Libya, political parties are illegal, and government officials under Mu'ammar al-Gadhafi hold tight control over any political activity that opposes Gadhafi's dictatorship. Citizens that attempt to form political parties are faced with severe prison terms and may even be sentenced to death. Like other totalitarian regimes, there is no freedom of the press. Libya's Al Ghad media group is tightly controlled by the government, as journalists work under extreme pressure of censorship and in an environment of fear. It is illegal to join or assemble in a group that is opposed to the government, and breaking this law carries the death penalty. No organizations that are independent from the government are allowed.

banned independent news organizations until only a handful of papers were left.[2] Iran fell in the rankings from the previous year as the government cracked down on journalists following the 2009 presidential election.

Freedom of Speech and the Right to Assemble

The US Constitution guarantees the freedom of speech, the right of people to assemble or hold meetings, and the right for people to request that the government listen to and respond to grievances. Totalitarian regimes severely curtail these basic personal freedoms in order to maintain tight control over people's actions against the ruling dictators or ruling parties.

Totalitarian regimes generally have a one-party system. Opposing political parties are banned or illegal. By curtailing the right to speech and to assemble, totalitarian regimes limit the people's ability to form political parties. Curtailing the right to assemble also limits civic groups, trade unions, special-interest groups, foundations, and professional organizations.

In democratic countries, people are allowed to form peaceful demonstrations if they are opposed to government policies. They engage in open public discussion and gather in groups to discuss political issues. In some totalitarian countries, freedom of assembly is not a constitutional right. An example of this is Cuba, where the government punishes the unauthorized assembly of more than three people. The government controls opposition by using state police and state security officials to harass and threaten people. It has the power to arrest and detain people as political prisoners without charging them with specific crimes. The Cuban constitution recognizes the Communist Party as the only legal party and "the superior leading force of society and of the state."[3] It claims to allow for freedom of speech and the press as long as people's views "conform to the aims of a socialist society."[4]

TIANANMEN SQUARE

In 1989, thousands of protestors, mostly students, gathered in Beijing and other cities in China in support of a democracy movement. Deng Xiaoping, the leader of China's Communist Party, had instituted a series of reforms called the Four Modernizations. These concentrated on improving agriculture, industry, science, and defense, but they did not include political reform. Student protestors and workers across the nation had been calling for political reform. Prodemocracy demonstrations were becoming more and more frequent.

The Chinese government chose to crack down on the demonstrations by sending in the military. On June 4, 1989, Chinese soldiers opened fire and tanks rolled over those who would not or could not get out of the way. No one knows for sure how many citizens were killed or wounded as the Chinese government has not released actual numbers, but there were reports of hundreds of dead. Following the incident, Chinese authorities repressed reports of the massacre. Deng accused the protestors of trying to overthrow the Communist Party and praised the action of the troops that put down the demonstration. Chinese leaders believed that it was necessary to put down the protestors in order to preserve the Communist Party's authority. Since 1989, some aspects of government control in China have loosened.

Due Process of Law and the Right to a Fair Trial

The US Constitution protects the rights of citizens who have been accused of crimes and guarantees citizens the right to a fair and speedy trial. In totalitarian regimes, people accused of crimes have few or no rights. Police are generally controlled by the ruling regime and can arrest people at will. Reporters and journalists are especially subjected to unlawful or lengthy imprisonments for publishing or writing about events a government wants to censor. By eliminating reporters through threats and harsh imprisonments, totalitarian governments prevent the general population from being informed. Many journalists have been jailed or even killed in their efforts to report news events. Ordinary citizens are often jailed for using the Internet or cell phones without permission, reading foreign publications, or listening to foreign radio stations. Other offenses, such as gathering in groups without permission, are designed to keep civil rights at a minimum and the population under control of the ruling powers. Civil rights such as trial by jury are often nonexistent for opposition activists who speak out against the government. In many cases, the judicial system is under the control of the ruling power. Prison conditions are harsh in many countries, and the sentences for crimes committed against the regime are often excessive and cruel.

In Cuba, political prisoners are denied fair trials, and an estimated 5,000 people have been convicted of "potential dangerousness."[5] Many of these people remain incarcerated in harsh conditions without being charged with any specific crimes. Prison conditions are harsh, and prisoners are often subjected to beatings by guards and denied adequate food, water, and medical help.

In Burma, citizens are persistently imprisoned for expressing their political views. Approximately 43 prisons hold political prisoners, and there are more than 50 labor camps in the country. A September 2009 Human Rights Watch report estimates that there are more than 2,100 political prisoners in Burma—more than double from early 2007.[6]

Totalitarian regimes of the past such as Stalin's Soviet Union, Hitler's Nazi Germany, and Mao's Communist China exiled people in harsh places such as Siberia or imprisoned them in labor or concentration camps. Similar camps exist today in countries such as North Korea,

NORTH KOREAN RESTRICTIONS

North Korea is one of the most restricted media environments in the world. It has a provision in its constitution that allows only government-sanctioned journalists to report news. The ruling party owns all the media and regulates all communication. Journalists are all members of the ruling party, and radio and television broadcasts work strictly as mouthpieces for government propaganda.

A law forbids listening to foreign radio and television and reading foreign publications. People who are caught are subject to severe punishments that include imprisonment, hard labor, or the death penalty. Foreign journalists are closely watched, and their ability to report and gather news is curtailed by government officials, who confiscate cell phones and prevent foreigners from talking to North Korean citizens.

where thousands of political prisoners are held under appalling conditions. Reports have been made that the government under Kim Jong Il has executed opponents of the regime as political prisoners without trials. In 2007, an addition to the country's penal code allowed for the execution of people found guilty of less serious crimes such as theft or cutting electric power or communication lines. People caught attempting to leave the country or helping others escape are also executed. Border guards are under orders to shoot and kill anyone attempting to cross the country's borders.

Civil liberties, such as freedom of speech, the press, and the right to assembly, are guaranteed by democratic governments. By denying these basic rights, dictators and ruling bodies of totalitarian regimes can further exert their hold and control over citizens. Other civil liberties such as the freedom to choose one's religion are also tightly controlled by totalitarian governments. ⌘

8

Religious Practice and Culture

Democratic countries generally protect the rights of individuals to choose their own religions. Many democratic countries, including the United States, guarantee that the state operates independently from any religion. In many totalitarian regimes, religious freedoms are curtailed, and in some cases, religions are banned. In totalitarian states where dictators have created cults of personality, religious beliefs are in direct conflict with the dictator's goals of achieving absolute rule and divine status. People are not only denied the freedom

Religious statues were removed from Buddhist temples during China's Cultural Revolution in 1966.

of choosing a religion, they are also prohibited from worshipping in religious buildings such as churches, temples, and mosques.

Communist Totalitarianism and Religion

In Communist totalitarian systems, there is no freedom of religion. Religious practice can interfere with the state ideology, so it is undesirable for citizens to have free choice of religion. Some Communist countries are officially atheist, meaning the people are not allowed to express a belief in God or a supreme being.

In the Soviet Union, Stalin closed tens of thousands of synagogues, churches, and mosques. Many religious leaders were arrested and put into prisons. By 1939, only a handful of Christian bishops were still active in the entire Soviet Union. Propaganda posters against religions began to appear all over the Soviet Union. The posters depicted religions as poisonous to children and illustrated religious holidays as the cause of fights or excessive drinking. To further weaken religious faiths, the Communist Party created a group called the League of Militant Atheists in 1924. The goal of the group was

"Religion is . . . the opium of the people."[1]

—*Karl Marx, coauthor of the* Communist Manifesto

to turn people away from religious beliefs and practices by organizing antireligious propaganda and burning icons and religious objects.

In Mao's China, many different religions were practiced, including Buddhism, Taoism, and Christianity. Following the Cultural Revolution, Communist leaders began to suppress the freedom of religion. Churches, temples, and monasteries were destroyed, or they lost their land and buildings to make room for agricultural space. Priests, monks, and other religious leaders were imprisoned or forced to leave the country. Some were forced to engage in nonreligious work.

THE KAZAN CATHEDRAL

Built in the seventeenth century, the Kazan Cathedral became a symbol of protection from Russia's enemies. Communists who sought to curtail religious freedom under Communist ideology destroyed the cathedral in 1936. Blueprints, photographs, and measurements of the building survived, however, and the cathedral was rebuilt and reopened in 1993 after the Soviet Union dissolved.

China has backed away from some of the more totalitarian aspects of its history. The country's government is authoritarian, but some freedoms are protected. In China today under the ruling Communist Party, religious practices and groups are somewhat tolerated. However, all religious groups must be registered with the

Chinese government. Only two Christian churches are recognized by the government, which controls church activities and interferes with religious studies and doctrine. Some religious groups are banned, such as certain Tibetan Buddhist and Uighur Muslim groups. Members of these groups often face persecution and, in some cases, imprisonment.

Cuba has also lessened its restrictions on religious activities in the last 20 years. In 1991, Cuba allowed Roman Catholics and other religious groups to join the Cuban Communist Party. The government, however, continues to interfere with certain religious matters despite the fact that the Cuban constitution recognizes the right of freedom of religion. Churches, for example, are not allowed to conduct educational activities because there are severe restrictions on academic freedom in Cuba. Church publications are controlled and monitored by the Office of Religious Affairs and are often subjected to censorship. The government also restricts the involvement of religious groups in institutions such as universities, hospitals, and nursing homes.

Totalitarianism and Theocracies

The word *theocracy* comes from the Greek words *theo* and *kratia*, which mean "God" and "rule" respectively. Therefore, in a theocratic state the law is dictated by religious beliefs. In countries such as these, religious leaders are the ruling powers of the government. The laws of a specific religion direct the laws of the state. There are few pure theocracies today, but many nations are guided by religious principles or religious leaders. Some of these countries use totalitarian methods to ensure their citizens adhere to their religious codes.

In Libya, Mu'ammar al-Gadhafi came to power in 1969 as the result of a military coup. The new government under the religious dictator took on the characteristics of a Fascist regime that combined the ideals of socialism, Islam, and Arab nationalism, which is the belief that all Arabs are united by a shared language, history, and culture. The Libyan government controls most aspects of its citizens' lives, and nearly all Libyans are Muslims.

Iran underwent a revolution in 1979, emerging as a tightly controlled theocracy. Religious leaders interpret Islamic law and enforce strict lifestyles on their citizens. In Iran in 1980, the Muslim cleric Ayatollah Ruholla Khomeini deposed Iran's monarchy and its leader, the Shah Mohammad Reza Pahlavi, who had adopted Western practices. Khomeini banned most Western practices and imposed strict Islamic law, called Sharia. People were no longer allowed to listen to Western music or wear Western clothing, and foreign magazines, books, music, and movies were banned. Islamic law required women to wear a form of dress in public covering their hair and entire bodies. In Iran today, some aspects of society have loosened, and some elements of Sharia are less strongly enforced. However, the government censors the press, the Internet, and broadcast media. In addition, journalists are subject to arrest for criticizing the government or its Islamic practices. Religious freedom is strictly limited to Islam, and religious leaders who stray from the official interpretation of the religion are subject to persecution.

Cultural Effects of Totalitarianism

Civil rights are severely restricted in totalitarian regimes. The objective of the dictator or ruling power is to uphold and maintain absolute power. The strict enforcement of the ruling power's ideologies also extends to the cultural arts, including music, literature, and paintings. Art and literature in particular are under close scrutiny in totalitarian regimes. All of the arts must reflect the regime in a positive manner, adding to the state-created propaganda.

Stalin believed the arts should serve his ideology of a Socialist state. In his attempt to control the arts, Stalin forced artists and writers to conform to a style of art that became known as social realism. In 1932, social realism became the official style of the regime. This style of art portrayed the ideals of socialism and communism in a positive light. Paintings were realistic and favored images of muscular, hardworking peasants portrayed in their collective-farm settings. Images of revolutionary heroes and of Stalin himself enhanced the dictator's cult of personality. Images of heroic acts and symbols such as beams of sunlight promoted hard work, a sense of nationalism, and a belief in a glorious future for the Soviet Socialist Republics. Many paintings in the style of social realism also depicted images of the hammer and sickle, the symbol of the Soviet

Union. Paintings of factories and agricultural landscapes were intended to glorify the accomplishments of the Soviet economy. Artists were not allowed to criticize the government through their works. Those who did were punished, and many were sent to labor camps in remote areas such as Siberia.

Writers and musicians were subject to the same scrutiny as artists. Books had to uphold hope in a Socialist future. The Soviet regime controlled which books were published, and authors who did not conform to the regime's ideology were punished by imprisonment, torture, or exile. For example, one of the country's most celebrated authors, Aleksandr Solzhenitsyn, was imprisoned in 1945 for writing letters to a friend that criticized Stalin. In 1953, he was sent into exile.

ANNA AKHMATOVA, RUSSIAN POET

Russian poet Anna Akhmatova (1889–1965) was most celebrated for her daring poem "Requiem," which described the suffering of the Soviet peasants under the dictatorship of Stalin. The poem was written as a result of the imprisonment of Akhmatova's son and the personal difficulty she encountered trying to visit him in prison. Her poems were banned from publication, and she was denounced by the Stalinist regime. It was not until 1987 that the poem "Requiem" was finally published in its entirety in the Soviet Union.

Mao's Four Olds Campaign and the Cultural Revolution

The effects of Mao Zedong's totalitarian rule also extended to the arts and literature. As in Stalin's social realism campaign, art, music, and literature had to serve the ideologies of the Chinese Communist Party. Artists and writers were persecuted if their works did not conform to Communist ideology or if they criticized the state. In the 1950s, Mao launched a campaign called the Four Olds Campaign. Its purpose was to eliminate old ideas, habits, customs, and cultures. Mao took the suppression of the arts even further. In 1966, he launched a campaign known as the Cultural Revolution. The campaign continued the Four Olds Campaign, but it also attacked universities, teachers, writers, and artists. It supported labor over education and sought to purge China of nonrevolutionary ways. The effect was catastrophic on the social, economical, and cultural elements of Chinese society.

The Chinese people were subjected to terror tactics by groups of revolutionary young people known as the Red Guards. These were mostly high school and university students recruited by Mao to attack people they thought threatened the Communist regime. The Red Guards, dressed in military uniforms and red armbands, roamed the streets and invaded homes, universities, and public buildings. They destroyed people's cherished possessions, clothing, and jewelry that represented old customs and culture. They stormed into universities and brutally beat teachers, injuring and killing tens of thousands.

Members of the Red Guard attended rallies to incite action in the Cultural Revolution.

During this period, the arts, music, and literature suffered tremendous losses. Precious works of art and cultural treasures were destroyed, books were burned, and musical instruments were smashed. Music and literature were banned. The destruction extended to the smashing and burning of temples, monasteries, and statues that honored family ancestors.

The Red Guards continued to terrorize China for several years. People suspected of threatening the revolution were targeted. Doctors, landlords, teachers, and writers were publicly humiliated, beaten, or killed. Millions of Chinese were killed or sent to labor camps. Many underwent reeducation, or thought reform, in which Communist party ideals were imposed on their thinking.

Schools and universities closed, and people lost their jobs. The violence and chaos was becoming so out of control that Mao finally put an end to the movement in 1969 by disbanding the Red Guards. Mao used the army to send millions of Red Guard members into the country to restore peace in the cities.

Religious freedoms are often denied in totalitarian regimes because the practice of religion and the corresponding beliefs take away from the ideology of the ruling regime. Dictators who have cultivated a cult of personality are threatened by religions, which interfere with the worship these leaders seek from citizens to maintain power. Likewise, freedom of expression in the arts does not always serve to put a ruling regime in a positive light. Totalitarian regimes depend on

THE LITTLE RED BOOK

Published in 1966, *The Little Red Book* served as a propaganda tool that enhanced Mao Zedong's personality cult. It was a collection of excerpts from hundreds of Mao's speeches and writings. The book's verses were memorized by millions of Chinese, who carried the book with them at all times. The sayings were intended to explain the ideology of the Chinese Communist Party and give people rules to live by.

sweeping away the past and replacing it with a new ideology. This destruction of history has often caused mass violence. ⌘

"[Our purpose is] to ensure that literature and art fit well into the whole revolutionary machine as a component part, that they operate as powerful weapons for uniting and educating the people and for attacking and destroying the enemy, and that they help the people fight the enemy with one heart and one mind."[2]

—*Mao Zedong*, The Little Red Book

9

Totalitarianism and the Economy

In a country with a free market economy, most businesses and industries are owned and controlled by individuals, not by the government. Consumer demand and the supply of goods determine prices for the most part. Most modern democratic governments are a combination of mixed economic systems in which a free market economy is supported by government regulations and actions. In the United States, the government is directly involved in decisions related to issues such as minimum wages, safe working conditions, and the safe production of food and drugs. Many

Totalitarian regimes control all aspects of their economies.

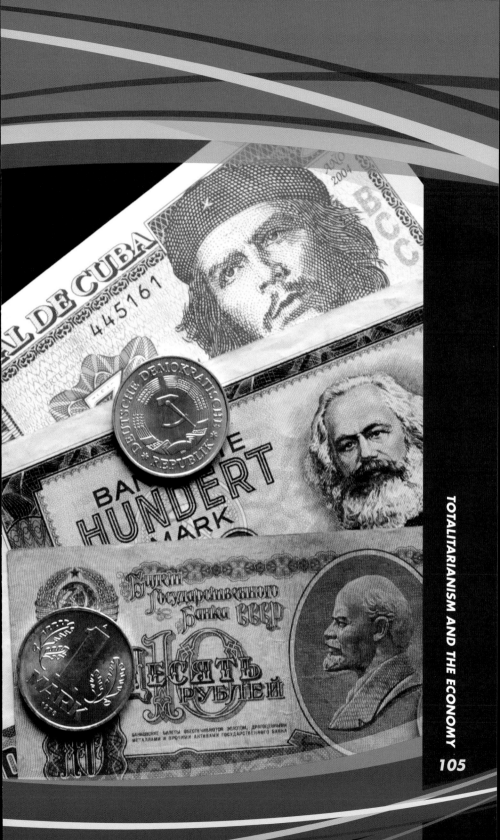

governments provide some level of health care, education, and retirement programs, such as Social Security, for citizens.

In totalitarian states, however, free market economies do not usually exist. Government control over business, agriculture, and industry can have a wide range of effects on their citizens, resulting in food shortages and economic depression. Totalitarian leaders can manipulate the economy to enrich themselves. On the other hand, the centralized control of a totalitarian government can result in increased employment and growing wealth.

Communist Totalitarianism and the Economy

Stalin rose to power in a country in which people suffered greatly from the effects of World War I and the Great Depression. Stalin wanted to establish a nation based on Socialist principles, which do not allow for a free economy. Instead, the Soviet economy would rely on public ownership of the means of production. That is, factories, mines, industry, and agriculture were to be run solely by the government. Businesses and banking systems were nationalized under Stalin. All private ownership of businesses and land was abolished, and people were required to work on state-owned farms or cooperatively run farms called collectives. Stalin and the Communist Party of the Soviet Union believed the means of production of goods belonged to the state, therefore they also believed the state should control all aspects of the economy.

Under Stalin, the industrial production of coal, steel, and electricity rose. An increase in production did not necessarily mean a better life for Soviet citizens, however. Working conditions remained dreadful because labor unions were outlawed, and there was not an increase of consumer goods such as food and clothing. The collective farming system brought disaster, resulting in famine and the deaths of millions.

World War II plunged the Soviet Union into further economic crises. New five-year plans after the war aimed to reconstruct the devastated nation by building up heavy industry. The military produced significant results as the Soviet Union began to emerge as a world power. After Stalin's death in 1953, Nikita Khrushchev emerged as Stalin's successor. Khrushchev's economic policies loosened the grip of the government, giving factories and farms more control over production.

As the Soviet Union became a modern industrial nation, it became a world power, building its military strength and numbers. The Soviet Union's production of steel, coal, oil, and electricity would continue to rise through the 1970s. However, consumer goods were often unavailable in the Soviet Union. Citizens often found themselves standing in long lines to buy goods and other household supplies. The Soviet Union could not match the standards of goods produced in Western countries, and products remained inferior. In addition, the collective agricultural system remained unproductive, resulting in food shortages. Continuing economic problems, among other factors, would lead to the collapse of the Soviet Union in 1991. However, the Soviet Union had impact on the economies of other Communist totalitarian regimes in the later part of the twentieth century.

PERESTROIKA

In the 1980s, Soviet leader Mikhail Gorbachev instituted an economic policy known as perestroika. This policy involved a restructuring of the Soviet economic system by modernizing it. The reforms, however, failed to increase the amount of goods available to the Soviet consumer, especially food. As a result, people were forced to wait in long lines to buy staple foods such as meat or bread. A huge black market economy emerged, selling these scarce goods at very high prices. The nation's deficit grew and economic growth declined. In 1991, Gorbachev resigned and the Soviet Union ceased to exist.

North Korea and Isolation

Like Stalin's and Khrushchev's policies in the Soviet Union, Kim Il Sung's Communist dictatorship affected North Korea's economy in various ways. North Korea was formed at the end of World War II when it was occupied by Soviet troops and Kim Il Sung rose to power. Kim Il Sung continued to align himself with the Soviet Union during and after the Korean War, which ended in 1953.

Kim began a policy of isolation from the rest of the world, establishing a philosophy of self-reliance known in Korean as *juche*. According to Kim's policy, the government of North Korea would be politically independent and economically self-sufficient. A strong military should enable the North Koreans to defend themselves without any outside aid. Under Kim's policies, the government did not engage other countries to invest in their resources or to trade with them, effectively cutting off the world.

However, North Korea traded with the Soviet Union and China and accepted Soviet and Chinese financial aid. Like Stalin's Soviet Union, the Communist government under Kim controlled all aspects of the economy. It owned and controlled all land, industries, businesses, and housing. The country concentrated its efforts on industrial growth and building a military. All farmland was organized into cooperatives. The government controlled agricultural practices, and it decided which crops to plant and where to plant them. Government interference and mismanagement resulted in a decrease in crop production.

To add to the country's woes, North Korea experienced a series of droughts and floods during the early 1990s that left its crops in ruins. The collapse of the Soviet Union added to the problems because North Korea was no longer receiving aid. The result was a massive famine in which nearly one million people were estimated to have died of starvation.[1] Kim ignored what was happening to the citizens of the country he ruled. As a result, the North Korean government did not ask for foreign aid, putting many more lives of its citizens at risk from the shortage of food. People were forced to eat grass and tree bark. The economic policy of Kim Il Sung was as disastrous as Stalin's agricultural policies that caused millions of Soviet deaths in the years prior to World War II.

The famine of the 1990s affected North Korea for much of the decade. Today, hunger and malnutrition among the North Korean people are still widespread. Because Kim Jong Il, the current dictator, still imposes a policy of juche, it is difficult for the rest of the world to assess what actually goes on inside the country's borders. Refugees who have escaped the country tell of stories of concentration camps and the difficult lives of the North Korean people.

THE INDEX OF ECONOMIC FREEDOM

The Index of Economic Freedom is a rating system that measures economic freedom in 183 countries around the world. Countries are rated on categories such as labor, business, trade, monetary, and investment freedoms as well as government spending and freedom from corruption. In 2010, the following totalitarian countries ranked in the bottom ten worst in terms of economic freedoms, with North Korea at the bottom of the list:

- 179 North Korea
- 178 Zimbabwe
- 177 Cuba
- 176 Eritrea
- 175 Burma
- 173 Libya
- 171 Turkmenistan[2]

Rich Leaders, Poor People

In totalitarian states, it is common for the party leaders to control much of the country's wealth, leaving many citizens in poverty. When the people of North Korea suffered from famine and the people of Cuba faced rationing, government officials continued to lead comfortable lives. The former leader of Turkmenistan, Saparmurat Niyazov, gutted his nation's economy in order to build large monuments to himself. In Zimbabwe, Robert Mugabe has been widely accused of manipulating the currency in order to enrich himself while children starved in the streets.

In Iraq, Saddam Hussein built eight luxurious palace compounds, which each contained mansions, guest villas, warehouses, office buildings, and garages. In all, the compounds contained more than 1,000 buildings. Hussein and his family lived a lavish lifestyle, but these palaces also had another function. British intelligence asserted that the compounds concealed secret weapons labs. Supposedly, Hussein built the labs within his palace compounds so he could keep international weapons inspectors out.

Totalitarian Regimes and Black Market Economies

Free market economies such as in the United States are based on the principle of supply and demand. Supply is the amount of a product or a service that is available on the free market. Demand is the amount of a product that buyers, or consumers, are willing to purchase. Supply and demand is directly related to the price of goods and services in a free-market economy. Countries such as the Soviet Union in the past and Cuba and North Korea today, whose governments spend heavily on industry and the military, often end up with a shortage of consumer goods. Because they lack everyday household items, the governments ration goods such as clothing, food, and soap. Electronics such as televisions, radios, and telephones are also in short supply.

Shortages of consumer goods can give rise to a black market economy, an economic climate in which goods or services are bought and sold illegally. Black market goods may also be illegal goods such as drugs or weapons. Other goods are sold on a black market to avoid taxes, such as firearms, alcoholic beverages, or cigarettes. When countries place restrictions on goods during times of rationing, or if these countries cannot keep up with the demand for goods, black markets develop. Some black market goods are less expensive than legal goods because they avoid taxes and other fees. Other black market goods are more expensive than they would be legally because they are scarce but in high demand. Black markets are found in all countries, but they can thrive under totalitarian systems due to inefficient economic policies of the government.

COST OF BLACK MARKET ITEMS IN BURMA

- Sport-utility vehicle: $250,000
- Cell phone: $2,500 to $3,000
- Gallon of gasoline: $5[3]

Burma's Black Market

As a result of the 1962 coup in Burma, the country became a totalitarian state in which the economy came under government control. Private industries were nationalized, and Burma's totalitarian regime called for a policy of self-reliance in which the country would manufacture and produce its own goods instead of importing goods from other countries. But because of ineffective and inefficient leadership, Burma's once-thriving economy plunged. There was a nationwide lack of consumer goods, and the government began to ration supplies because of low industrial output. Because the government rationed essential items such as gasoline, rice, and oil, government stores often had empty shelves.

By 1987, Burma was ranked as one of the world's poorest countries. Severe droughts caused a bad harvest, and a shortage of rice meant a shortage of food. In that year, the United Nations listed Burma as a "Least Developed Country," which meant that the average Burmese citizen made less than $200 per year.[4]

In addition, due to Burma's deplorable human rights conditions, the United States in 2003 imposed sanctions on Burma, banning Burmese products from being imported into the United States. The United States and other countries also placed economic sanctions on the totalitarian regime. That is, most countries will not give the Burmese government financial aid. Because of the unavailability of consumer goods, a huge black market developed in Burma.

Cars and transportation systems are out-dated, and much of the country is in a state of disrepair. Most Burmese citizens are forced to buy items on the black market because they cannot find goods in stores or markets. Everyday products and goods such as electronic equipment, clothing, soap, cosmetics, and medicine are smuggled into Burma from Thailand, China, and other countries. Traders bribe officials on both sides of the borders to bring in goods. The goods are then sold for extremely high prices or traded for Burma's natural resources, including precious gems and teak forest products. Burma also has an active illegal drug trade, and it is the second-highest producer of opium in the world.

Totalitarian governments can have a variety of effects on the economy of a nation depending on how the government manages the economy. As in Stalin's Soviet Union, a strong central government can improve a country's industry, even if it is at the expense of its people. A centralized

BURMA'S ILLEGAL DRUG TRADE

Burma is the second-highest producer of illegal opium and cultivator of opium poppy plants. In 2008, the country produced an estimated 375 tons (340 metric tonnes) of opium.[5] Government corruption and inefficiency has resulted in a lack of commitment by the government to stop drug trafficking and to fight against major narcotics groups.

economy such as in North Korea can have devastating effects on its citizens. Some dictators choose to exploit their country's resources for their own personal wealth. Mismanagement of the economy can result in failed crops, famine, depression, or the rise of illegal black markets. ⌘

10

Daily Life

Citizens in totalitarian countries lack basic civil liberties. Economic policies affect how people live and work and the amount of goods and services available. Although daily life varies from country to country, many of the citizens of totalitarian countries share common problems caused by economic troubles and the lack of civil rights.

In totalitarian countries, most citizens struggle daily to put food on the table and buy the basic necessities of life. There is little in the way of luxuries, as those are reserved for the ruling powers and their supporters. Adults must live where the government tells them to, and

During food shortages in Cuba, citizens wait in long lines for their rations of fish, fruit, and vegetables.

they often cannot find work of their choice. Often, public transportation is haphazard and the ownership of private cars or other vehicles is rare. Most citizens are not allowed to leave the country or to make contact with the outside world. In many places, traveling around within the country is also restricted. In countries such as North Korea, people who are caught leaving or who are brought back into the country after escaping are subject to imprisonment and torture.

Life under Castro

In many totalitarian states, food and goods shortages are common due to government interference and inefficiency. Because of this, some countries, such as Cuba, have had to ration food and consumer goods. A 16-year-old refugee described life in Cuba under Castro in the 1990s:

> *In Cuba, the government controls your life. Everything is rationed. Each family has a little booklet called a "libreta" with coupons in it. You want to buy a pair of pants? You can't just run over to . . . some shopping center. In Cuba, each family is assigned a special week to shop for clothes, say, May 21 to May 28 . . . You're supposed to go on those days to get what the coupons say, maybe one skirt or one shirt. You get one pair of shoes for one year. Even underwear is rationed, three pairs for each person for one year.*[1]

It is no small wonder that in the years following Castro's coup in 1959, hundreds of thousands of Cubans have immigrated to the United States,

many by boats, making a desperate and danger-
ous crossing between Cuba and the shores of
Florida. Daily life in Cuba has been difficult
and oppressive. Its citizens have survived with
a poor standard of living ever since the loss of
Soviet aid with the collapse of the Soviet Union
in 1991. Along with clothing, the government
rations food and other household products. Many
Cubans who live in the United States send their
relatives letters and money to buy goods. But
some of the letters never reach their destinations
because Cuban officials sometimes open letters
and confiscate US currency.

Work, Education, and the Cult of Personality

In some totalitarian regimes, the government
even decides a person's vocation. The government controls salaries and wages. Families often
do not earn enough to make ends meet. Trade
unions are outlawed and working conditions are
often poor, difficult, and unsanitary. Workers are
not allowed to go on strike, and negotiation for
higher wages and better working conditions is
unheard of. People who try to improve working
conditions or organize labor unions are subject to
harassment or even imprisonment.

Children receive education, but the state
regulates what subjects are taught, and they are
indoctrinated in the particular ideology of the
totalitarian regime. However, some countries,
such as China, have improved literacy rates
under dictatorship. Under Mao, the Chinese

government implemented programs to encourage literacy, mainly because they wanted the people to be able to read government propaganda.

Sports and cultural activities, like everything else, are regulated by the state, but in today's China and formerly in the Soviet Union, youth who have sports skills have been encouraged to develop those talents. Both China and the former Soviet Union have been internationally recognized as powerhouses in the Olympic Games. China made a huge effort to build national pride through the sport of table tennis. Table tennis even forged a diplomatic bridge between China and the United States at the World Table Tennis Championship in 1971.

In 1974, North Korea's Kim Il Sung announced the Ten Principles for the Establishment of the One-Ideology System, a set of rules that North Koreans must follow in their daily lives. Every North Korean citizen must know the Ten Principles and recite the rules on

THE *RUHNAMA*

Under the totalitarian regime of Turkmenistan's former dictator Saparmurat Niyazov, all citizens were required to read and study a book he wrote called the *Ruhnama.* The book was intended to provide spiritual and moral guidance for Turkmenistan's citizens. Under Niyazov's rule, the text was mandatory reading in all classrooms. The book added to the huge cult of personality created by the dictator in the 1990s.

a daily basis. The basic rules are supported by a set of articles that further explain the principles of the rules. One article expressly instructs that all North Koreans must gather every two days to two weeks for evaluation meetings in which they must examine if they have followed the rules or not. North Korean citizens also must have a portrait of their "Great Leader" in their homes.

KIM IL SUNG'S TEN PRINCIPLES

Rules from the North Korean dictator's Ten Principles for the Establishment of the One-Ideology System:

Rule 1. *We must give our all in the struggle to unify the entire society with the revolutionary ideology of the Great Leader Kim Il Sung.*

Rule 2. *We must honor the Great Leader comrade Kim Il Sung with all our loyalty.*

Rule 4. *We must make the Great Leader comrade Kim Il Sung's revolutionary ideology our faith and make his instructions our creed.*

Rule 7. *We must learn from the Great Leader comrade Kim Il Sung and adopt the Communist look,*

revolutionary work methods, and people-oriented work style.

Rule 10. *We must pass down the great achievement of the revolution by the Great Leader comrade Kim Il Sung from generation to generation, inheriting and completing it to the end.*[2]

Article 3, Paragraph 3 of the Ten Principles states:

> All portraits, plaster casts, statues of comrade Kim Il Sung, publications holding a portrait of the Great Leader, works of art depicting the Great Leader, message boards displaying sayings of the Great Leader and the basic principles of the Party must be enshrined and strictly protected.[3]

Life inside the Home

Restrictions on personal freedoms in totalitarian regimes do not just exist outside the home. Television and radio stations are fixed to state channels, which are used as mouthpieces for a regime's political ideologies. Telephone connections are limited, and most totalitarian regimes do not allow phone calls outside of the country. Countries such as Burma have telephone systems that are underdeveloped: only one of every 100 Burmese citizens has telephone service.[4] Even the use of cell phones is restricted. Countries such as North Korea carry severe penalties for people caught using telephones to contact the outside world.

There are also severe restrictions on the Internet. Foreign Web sites are blocked, and those people who have Internet access are closely monitored for evidence of opposition to the ruling powers or dictator. Many citizens in totalitarian countries are not even allowed to have Internet access, or it is a privilege for the few. Many people, such as citizens in Cuba,

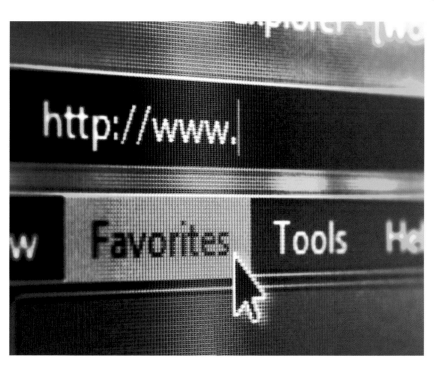

In China, Internet usage is restricted by the government.

simply cannot afford it. In contrast, China has the largest number of Internet users in the world, with almost 300 million users.[5] However, the government blocks Web sites and removes Web sites it considers politically threatening.

In 2009, the Chinese government announced it would require the installation of censorship and surveillance software on all computers sold in China. The software was called the Green Dam Youth Escort. The government relaxed its position under pressure from international communities, human rights groups, and Internet users, but the government still requires the installation of the software in schools and Internet cafés.

In some ways, family life for most people is similar to life in democratic countries. Families have the same concerns: finding work, raising children, and keeping food on the table. Families in totalitarian countries, however, are less mobile. Some countries forbid travel or make it very difficult to get permission. In countries with secret police, neighbors are often wary of each other, for fear of having their activities reported to the authorities. Democracies are more likely to have diverse populations with people of different ethnicities and religions mixing together. Some historic totalitarian states, such as Mao's China, disrupted families in pursuit of the regime's greater goals.

INFANTICIDE IN CHINA

In China, it is socially desirable to have male babies. The enforcement of the one child per family rule has resulted in the practice of infanticide, or killing, of baby girls. Girls are often sent to orphanages, resulting in many overseas adoptions. The overall result of the one child per family rule in China has been a population with a shortage of women.

China instituted a law in the 1980s that restricted married couples to having one child. Since 1949, due to better living conditions and health care, the population of China has grown to 1.3 billion people, and the huge population presents challenges as well as a multitude of problems for the future. Families with more than one child face fines or penalties.

Civic life in totalitarian countries has many challenges. A lack of civil rights is frequently coupled with a bad economy. Often, personal freedoms such as choosing a career or deciding where to live are restricted. Academic freedoms suffer, and extreme measures to indoctrinate citizens can creep into a person's personal life and home. ⌘

11

International Relations

The international relations of totalitarian regimes can have an effect on the daily lives of their citizens and can also affect other countries throughout the world. A totalitarian regime's trade policy affects its economy and the economies of other countries. The regime's policies on nuclear weapons may pose a threat to the security of other countries. A country with a poor human rights record might provoke censure from the international community.

The United Nations is one international organization that works to bring democracy to totalitarian countries.

World Powers, Trade, and Nuclear Weapons

The importing and exporting of goods stimulates a nation's economy and can increase its wealth. Nations can export resources or products to other countries and import products or resources that are not readily available internally. For example, many countries do not have rich oil reserves, so they must import such resources from oil-producing countries.

Countries with little wealth or economic growth, such as Burma, lack both resources to export and wealth to import necessary resources. As a result, people are left without many of the necessities of daily life. Foreign investors are reluctant to invest in businesses or industry in Burma because of the amount of corruption in the government. Burma does have a rich supply of natural gas, which it exports, but it must import crude oil and diesel fuel. Crude oil and diesel fuel are both prevalent on the Burmese black market.

North Korea is in a similar situation. The government makes it difficult for foreign businesses to invest in the country, and foreign businesses are wary of government corruption. Trade with other countries is almost nonexistent due to the Kim Jong Il policy of juche, or self-reliance. As a result, North Korea lacks the wealth necessary to import adequate oil. Farming is unproductive without fuel for machinery, factories are shut down or their hours are shortened, and people go for long hours at home without electric light or heat.

During the famine of the 1990s, North Korea requested food supplies from the international community. The United States, Japan, and South Korea sent massive supplies of food, but the government interfered with its distribution, and it is believed that much of the food supplies never reached hungry North Korean citizens. In 2008, the United States agreed to send 551,000 tons (500,000 metric tonnes) of food via the World Food Organization, but the North Korean government stopped additional shipments in March 2009.[1] Today, Kim Jong Il's regime continues to build an arsenal of nuclear weapons at the expense of his nation, which cannot feed itself.

World powers such as the former Soviet Union and present-day China have had a huge impact on international relations. In China, US President Richard Nixon's visit in 1972 began to open up the Communist country's diplomatic ties with

REFUGEES

Many refugees have escaped countries such as Burma, North Korea, and Cuba and sought asylum in other countries around the world. An estimated 30,000 to 50,000 people have illegally entered China from North Korea. China has tried to stop North Korean refugees by building a fence along parts of the shared border. In North Korea, people deported back into the country from China face imprisonment and harsh punishments.[2]

the United States. By the end of the 1970s, the United States had established full diplomatic relations with China, and China itself was becoming a world superpower. Businesses in the United States saw opportunities for trade and investment as the Chinese economy under the leadership of Deng Xiaoping continued to grow. However, relations between the United States and China were strained due to China's treatment of its own citizens and the brutal killing of prodemocracy demonstrators in China's capital of Beijing at Tiananmen Square in 1989. China also continued to sell nuclear arms and other weapons to countries the United States considered hostile, including Iran. In the twenty-first century, China has continued to build its arsenal of weapons and grow its military.

Economic Sanctions

Nations that disagree with the way a dictatorship or totalitarian regime violates human rights, uses nuclear arms, or implements other repressive policies sometimes impose sanctions against that government. Sanctions consist of cutting off trade and business relations with a country. Imports, exports, and financial loans are put to an end, with the goal of getting a repressive regime to change its policies by hurting its economy.

The United States has imposed sanctions on many different repressive regimes in the past, such as China, Vietnam, Cuba, Iran, Libya, North Korea, and Iraq. Sanctions can affect a government in different ways. For example, the economic sanctions imposed on Iraq by the

China maintains a strong army.

United Nations (UN) in the 1990s were designed to hinder the progress of Iraq's weapons of mass destruction, including nuclear, biological, and chemical weapons. Dictator Saddam Hussein, whose policies led to the murder of Iraqi citizens, ignored the UN weapons ban and interfered with weapons inspectors sent to Iraq. After several years, some Middle Eastern countries began to trade with Iraq, and the effectiveness of the sanctions was diminished.

Eventually, Hussein's regime was toppled by the invasion of coalition forces led by the United States in 2003. Outside interference by other countries is a common way for totalitarian regimes to fall. Hitler and Mussolini were both ousted by war; other times, foreign countries covertly help rebels overthrow their governments.

NUCLEAR NON-PROLIFERATION TREATY

The Nuclear Non-Proliferation Treaty is a legal commitment among nations of the world. It fosters international cooperation to stop the spread of nuclear weapons. The treaty was opened for signature in July 1968 and has since been signed by 190 countries.[3] The goal of the treaty is threefold: countries with nuclear weapons will reduce them, countries without nuclear weapons will not attempt to acquire them, and all countries are allowed to use nuclear power peacefully as a source of energy.

North Korea and Nuclear Arms

North Korea has been pursuing a program of nuclear weapons for many years, announcing for the first time in 2002 that the government possessed nuclear weapons. At the time, North Korea had signed the Nuclear Non-Proliferation Treaty, which limits the spread, or proliferation, of nuclear weapons. North Korea withdrew from the treaty, claiming the United States did not live up to its end of an earlier agreement. As a result of North Korea's withdrawal from the Non-Proliferation Treaty, a series of negotiations called the Six-Party Talks began in 2003 among North Korea, South Korea, China, the

United States, Japan, and the Russian Federation. The goal of the talks was to end North Korea's nuclear program. Since the talks began, there have been several rounds of negotiations, but the talks have failed to end North Korea's nuclear weapons program.

In October 2006, the North Korean government announced that it had successfully conducted an underground nuclear test for the first time. Seismic tests conducted by Japan and the United States confirmed the report. In May 2009, North Korea conducted another nuclear test. Reports surfaced that Kim Jong Il's regime had achieved the status of a full-fledged nuclear power. The future of North Korea's nuclear weapons program remains to be seen as diplomatic negotiations continue.

Democratic nations worry about nuclear weapons in the hands of totalitarian regimes such as North Korea. Nuclear weapons might fall into the hands of unstable or hostile governments. They might be used to threaten the United States or other democratic governments. In addition, nuclear weapons could be sold to independent terrorist groups or used to support their actions.

Human Rights and the United Nations

The UN was founded in 1945 after the end of World War II. The goal of the 51 countries that formed the UN was to promote world peace through cooperation among nations. It adopted the Universal Declaration of Human Rights in 1948. The document outlined the basic human rights that the UN agreed every person should have. Despite this international agreement, totalitarian regimes continue to deny basic human rights to their citizens. The UN General Assembly has condemned human right abuses in nations such as North Korea. The General Assembly has also reacted to the detention and violence against foreign journalists in Zimbabwe following the 2008 elections and condemned Burma for ordering its army to fire on student prodemocracy demonstrations in 1988 and killing approximately 3,000 people.[4]

The work of the United Nations has helped to promote and advance the cause of human rights such as freedom of speech, the press, and religion. It promotes the right of every person to food, education, adequate housing, and medical treatment. It works to protect people against

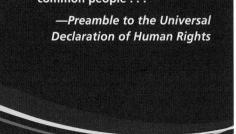

"Whereas recognition of the inherent dignity and of the equal and inalienable rights of all members of the human family is the foundation of freedom, justice and peace in the world,

"Whereas disregard and contempt for human rights have resulted in barbarous acts which have outraged the conscience of mankind, and the advent of a world in which human beings shall enjoy freedom of speech and belief and freedom from fear and want has been proclaimed as the highest aspiration of the common people . . ."[5]

—*Preamble to the Universal Declaration of Human Rights*

arbitrary detention, torture, and execution. In addition, it also works to protect the rights of women, children, and minority groups who might be subject to injustices under totalitarian regimes.

Nations working together through the UN or other groups have improved the lives of people who suffer under totalitarian or other kinds of repressive regimes. For example, the organization Amnesty International works to investigate and report on human rights abuses around the world. The United States broadcasts the radio station Voice of America into totalitarian and nondemocratic countries to provide citizens with news from the outside world. The nations of the world send aid to poverty-stricken people around the world, even to countries ruled by totalitarian dictators. With pressure from international communities and organizations, lives of repressed people have improved, but there is still a long way to go and much to be accomplished. ⌘

12

The Many Faces of Totalitarianism

Despite the differences that exist among totalitarian regimes of the present and the past, all of these countries have several characteristics in common. Totalitarian regimes consist of a single party led by a leader or group that mobilizes an entire country in support of an official state ideology, or a set of ideas that explains a political agenda such as communism or nationalism. Activities that are in opposition to the state or its goals are not tolerated, and the ruling power controls the economic policies, religion, political parties, and activities of its

Burma supporters in San Francisco, California, carried signs bringing attention to the human rights violations in Burma.

citizens. The state enforces its control of citizens through the widespread use of terror tactics by regular police and by secret police.

Totalitarianism is a phenomenon of the twentieth century, due in part to the development of technologies such as television, radio, and film. These allow totalitarian dictators to address citizens directly, spreading propaganda and their totalitarian ideologies. It also enables totalitarian dictators to develop personality cults. The most repressive of totalitarian regimes withhold civil and human rights from their citizens.

Pros and Cons and Strengths and Weaknesses

Just as every coin has two sides, so every totalitarian regime has its strengths and weaknesses. What will history's verdict be of leaders such as Hitler, Stalin, and Mao? It is documented that all three of these leaders brought hardship and death to millions of citizens and subjected millions more to unjust imprisonment. Certainly, human rights were violated at all levels. But there were certain achievements under their leadership. Hitler brought his country out of severe economic depression, building industries and creating jobs for the unemployed. Stalin's five-year plans revolutionized a nation of peasants and turned the Soviet Union into a leading world power. Soviet technological and industrial development that occurred prior to 1941 enabled the Soviets to help defeat Nazi Germany in World War II. Under Mao, an undeveloped and poverty-stricken peasant society was industrialized, and its people were given educational opportunities. By the 1950s in China and the Soviet Union, many people received better housing, education, and medical care than in previous decades. However, their inefficient economic systems did little to improve the quality of life, eliminating private ownership and personal freedoms. Workers in industrial settings were not motivated under a system that did not allow for rewards, benefits, or increases in pay. Production and the quality of products suffered as a consequence. Citizens suffered repression, and millions died under each of these regimes. These leaders' accomplishments came at a high cost.

CHINA AND HUMAN RIGHTS

Harry Wu is a human rights activist who was imprisoned in China for 19 years for criticizing the Chinese Communist regime. He refers to the Chinese labor camps as *laogai*, noting that much of the nation's economy and production is based on the work of prisoners in labor camps. Wu notes: "The laogai is not simply a prison system, it is a political tool for maintaining the Communist Party's totalitarian rule."[1]

In today's world, serious violations of human rights are rampant in regimes such as Burma, China, North Korea, Zimbabwe, and Cuba, to name a few. Despite the humanitarian efforts of international organizations and democratic countries around the world, the repression of civic and human rights continues. People who are arrested as political prisoners for opposing the government suffer under harsh and brutal conditions. They have few or no rights under constitutions that are not upheld. Some countries have no working constitution at all. Unlike totalitarian regimes of the past, there is little improvement in the quality of the lives of citizens under the regimes of Kim Jong Il, Robert Mugabe, or Burma's military junta. Many nations under the rule of totalitarian leaders are among the most impoverished nations in the world. For example, in Zimbabwe, 68 percent of its citizens live below the poverty line.[2] In Burma, 32.7 percent live below the poverty line.[3] And in Turkmenistan the number is 30 percent.[4] In China, however, only 2.8 percent of its citizens live below the poverty line due to China's rapidly growing economy and greater economic freedoms.[5]

However, totalitarian regimes give a nation an element of stability. A collapse of the regime in North Korea, for example, might result in a massive outpouring of refugees, military disorder, and the rise of gangs and local warlords. In addition, internal chaos could result in a loss of government control over military weapons. The consequences of military or nuclear weapons in the wrong hands could have devastating results internationally. Similar situations could certainly occur in other totalitarian regimes in other parts of the world. Countries with little preparation for democratic freedoms and processes could be subject to chaos and anarchy.

The Call for Democracy

At the start of the twentieth century, monarchies and empires ruled the world. There were only 55 sovereign states worldwide, compared to approximately 200 in 2010. Only a few countries, such as the United States and Great Britain, had democratic systems. At the end of World War II, there were 22 democracies worldwide and about the same number with partial democratic practices.[6] Communist regimes spread to different nations. Since the 1970s, however, the number of democratic nations has increased and the number of dictatorships has decreased. Despite the

ERITREA IN TRANSITION

The country of Eritrea gained independence from Ethiopia in 1993. Outside observers, as well as the people of the new nation, hoped the country would avoid a dictatorship. During these years, it remained a nation in transition as the government moved away from a Communist ideology. However, Eritrea has remained an authoritarian state under the leadership of the People's Front for Democracy and Justice (PFDJ), which is its only political party. Eritrea has a constitution that is not enforced, and its citizens have few civil rights. The government controls the economy even though it claims to support a free market and private enterprise. Elections in Eritrea have been indefinitely postponed, and Eritrea remains in border disputes with its neighbor Ethiopia.

repressiveness of totalitarian regimes, prodemocracy protests take place in these countries and in dictatorships all over the world. As more countries move toward electoral democracy, it becomes more difficult for totalitarian regimes to isolate themselves from the world. In some cases, popular movements can lead to democracy. In other cases, totalitarian regimes maintain or even strengthen their hold.

Today, citizens living in totalitarian states continue to live under harsh and repressive governments. However, international organizations, the UN, and democratic countries continue to press for democracy. Leaders such as Aung San Suu Kyi, who has fought for freedom in Burma, continue to inspire people to fight against tyrannical regimes. Her words, from her work *Freedom From Fear*, describe how both fear and courage play a part under an oppressive totalitarian government:

IS IT DEMOCRACY?

A democratic country such as the United States has laws that some people might feel violate personal freedoms. Do seat belt laws requiring people to wear seat belts in their cars interfere with personal freedom? Security cameras are everywhere to protect citizens, but do they also interfere with an individual's right to privacy? These questions undergo fierce debate. But in the United States, unlike totalitarian states, people are guaranteed the right to challenge and oppose the government.

Within a system that denies the existence of basic human rights, fear tends to be the order of the day. Fear of imprisonment, fear of torture, fear of death, fear of losing friends, family, property, or means of livelihood, fear of poverty, fear of isolation, fear of failure . . . It is not easy for a people conditioned by the iron rule of the principle that might is right to free themselves from the [draining atmosphere] of fear. Yet even under the most crushing state machinery courage rises up again and again, for fear is not the natural state of civilized man.[7] ⌘

Quick Facts

Definition of Totalitarianism

A totalitarian society is one in which a ruling power, such as a dictator or a political party, has almost complete control over the government and all of its activities, as well as all aspects of the lives of the individual citizen. The ruling dictator has control of the economy, and the military and all businesses and industries are nationalized. The dictator supports an ideology such as communism or fascism that forms the ideology of the state. The government controls the media and press, and there are few, if any, civil liberties. Propaganda, secret police, and terror tactics are used to control the citizens of the state.

Well-Known Totalitarian Countries

Burma, Cuba, North Korea, Zimbabwe

Organization of Totalitarian States

The leader or ruling group controls all power. If there are branches of the government, they are all subordinate to the leader.

Main Leadership Positions

- Dictator: ruling leader with absolute power, often controls by force

- Military junta: a government run by military leaders and controlled by force

Historic Leaders

- Joseph Stalin, United Soviet Socialist Republics (1922–1953): first general secretary of the Soviet Union's Communist Party

- Benito Mussolini, Italy (1922–1945): leader of the National Fascist Party

- Adolf Hitler, Germany (1933–1945): leader of the National Socialist German Workers Party

- Mao Zedong, China (1949–1976): revolutionary Communist leader

How Power Shifts

- Appointment: Adolf Hitler (Germany), Benito Mussolini (Italy)
- Coup d'état: Burma, Cuba
- Inheritance of power: North Korea
- Death of dictator: Joseph Stalin (Soviet Union), Mao Zedong (China)

Economic Systems

- Central economies: one in which the government controls all businesses and industry (Cuba, North Korea, former Soviet Union).
- Collective farms: a system of agriculture in which the state owns all farms and people live and work on farms collectively, sharing the work and housing. All products are given to the government (China, former Soviet Union).

The Roles of Citizens

Citizens have little or no participation in government unless they are members of the single party that leads the state and work for the controlling dictator.

Personal Freedoms and Rights

There are no civil rights or personal freedoms. Totalitarian states do not allow freedom of speech, the press, assembly, or religion. Citizens are not allowed to oppose the government or form opposing political parties.

Strengths of Totalitarianism

- Can nationalize a country
- Develops industries and technology
- Improves literacy rates
- Improves standard of living, including education and health care
- Provides citizens with jobs and housing

Weaknesses of Totalitarianism

- Takes away civil rights and personal freedoms
- Encourages human rights abuses such as harsh prison camps
- Destroys economy resulting in depression or famine
- Does not allow people a say in government
- Does not allow people to leave the country

Glossary

Aryan
Person of North European descent.

asylum
Protection granted by a country to a person who has left his or her own country as a political refugee.

authoritarian
Nondemocratic rule by a state authority.

collectivize
To put all economic activity under the control of the state.

commune
A community whose members share everything in common.

communism
The economic and political system based on collective ownership of property and equal distribution of goods.

constitution
A written document that sets forth the fundamental principles or precedents that govern a state or organization.

coup
A sudden and usually violent overthrow of a government.

defection
Abandonment of one's native country.

democracy
A form of government that is ruled by the people.

dictator
Leader who rules a country with absolute power, usually with force.

fascism
A political philosophy that exalts the leader or a group of people over the individual; characterized by dictatorial rule, oppression, and the forceful stopping of resistance.

ideology
A system of ideas or beliefs that form the basis of an economic or political system or policy.

indoctrination
The teaching or forcing of a set of beliefs on a person.

junta
A military or political group that imposes rule over a country after taking control by force.

military
Soldiers and armed forces of a country.

propaganda
Information intended to mislead or influence and promote a particular political cause or point of view.

regime
A ruling government.

revolution
Forcible overthrow of a government or social order in favor of a new system.

Sharia
Islamic law based on the Koran.

socialism
An economic system based on collective or state ownership of industry and business.

theocracy
A government in which rulers are believed to be guided by the divine.

trade union
An organization whose main purpose is to help workers receive fair wages, benefits, and decent working conditions in a particular trade or industry.

Additional Resources

Selected Bibliography

"Background Notes." *US Department of State.* US Department of State, 23 Apr. 2010. Web.

Brooks, Jeffrey. *Thank You, Comrade Stalin!* Princeton, NJ: Princeton UP, 2000. Print.

Peloso, Jennifer, editor. *The Two Koreas.* New York: H. W. Wilson, 2004. Print.

Wakeman, Carolyn, and San San Tin. *No Time for Dreams.* New York: Rowman, 2009. Print.

"The World Factbook." *Central Intelligence Agency.* Central Intelligence Agency, 29 Sept. 2010. Web.

"Worst of the Worst: The World's Most Repressive Societies 2009." *Freedom House.* Freedom House, 2009. Web.

Further Readings

Cunningham, Kevin. *Joseph Stalin and the Soviet Union.* Greensboro, NC: Morgan Reynolds, 2006. Print.

Demick, Barbara. *Nothing to Envy: Ordinary Lives in North Korea.* New York: Spiegel, 2010. Print.

Geyer, Flora. *Mao Zedong: The Rebel Who Led a Revolution.* Washington, DC: National Geographic, 2007. Print.

Larkin, Emma. *Finding George Orwell in Burma.* New York: Penguin, 2006. Print.

Orwell, George. *1984.* New York: Plume, 2003.

Web Links

To learn more about totalitarianism, visit ABDO Publishing Company online at **www.abdopublishing.com**. Web sites about totalitarianism are featured on our Book Links page. These links are routinely monitored and updated to provide the most current information available.

Places to Visit

United Nations Headquarters Building
First Avenue and Forty-Sixth Street
New York, NY 10017
212-963-8687
www.un.org
The United Nations Headquarters Building is open to the public with tours available.

United States Holocaust Memorial Museum
100 Raoul Wallenberg Place SW
Washington, DC 20024-2126
202-488-0400
www.ushmm.org
The Holocaust Memorial Museum features exhibits related to World War II, Hitler, and the Holocaust.

Source Notes

Chapter 1. What Is Totalitarianism?

1. "KGB." *Encyclopedia Britannica.* Encyclopedia Britannica Online, 2010. Web. 14 Oct. 2010.

2. "Worst of the Worst: The World's Most Repressive Societies 2009." *Freedom House.* Freedom House, 2009. Web. 14 Oct. 2010.

3. Benito Mussolini. "Doctrine of Fascism (1932)." *The History Guide: Lectures on Twentieth-Century Europe.* Steven Kreis, 2004. Web. 14 Oct. 2010.

4. "Worst of the Worst: The World's Most Repressive Societies 2009." *Freedom House.* Freedom House, 2009. Web. 14 Oct. 2010.

Chapter 2. Fascism in Europe

1. "WWI Casualty and Death Tables." *The Great War and the Shaping of the 20th Century.* PBS, 2004. Web. 14 Oct. 2010.

2. "Global Alert and Response: Pandemic Preparedness." *World Health Organization.* WHO, 2010. Web. 14 Oct. 2010.

3. "The Individual Soldier." *Intelligence Bulletin* 1.4 (Dec. 1942): N. pag. *The Lone Sentry.* Web. 14 Oct. 2010.

4. Ibid.

5. Erika Mann. *School for Barbarians.* New York: Modern Age, 1938. *Facing History and Ourselves.* Web. 14 Oct. 2010.

Chapter 3. Communism and Totalitarian Dictators

1. Lyons, Eugene. *Assignment in Utopia.* New York: Harcourt Brace, 1937. Print. 280.

2. "Ukrainian Famine." *Revelations from the Russian Archives.* Library of Congress, 22 July 2010. Web. 14 Oct. 2010.

3. Michael Schoenhals. *China's Cultural Revolution, 1966–1969: Not a Dinner Party.* New York: M. E. Sharp, 1996. 106. *Google Book Search.* Web. 14 Oct. 2010.

4. Nicholas Eberstadt "The Great Leap Backward." Rev. of *Hungry Ghosts: Mao's Secret Famine,* by Jasper Becker. *New York Times On the Web.* New York Times Company, 16 Feb. 1997. Web. 14 Oct. 2010.

5. Arifa Akbar. "Mao's Great Leap Forward 'Killed 45 Million in Four Years.'" *The Independent.* independent.co.uk, 17 Sept. 2010. Web. 14 Oct. 2010.

6. Robert Payne. *Mao Tse-Tung Ruler of Red China*. Read Books, 2008. *Google Book Search*. Web. 14 Oct. 2010.

Chapter 4. The Exchange of Power

1. "Freedom in the World—Burma (Myanmar) (2010)." *Freedom House*. Freedom House, 2010. Web. 14 Oct. 2010.

2. "Countdown to Freedom: Aung San Suu Kyi Must Be Released On November 13, 2010." *Freedom Now*. Freedom Now, 2010. 14 Oct. 2010.

3. Gustaaf Houtman. *Mental Culture in Burmese Crisis Politics: Aung San Suu Kyi and the National League for Democracy.* Tokyo: Institute for the Study of Languages and Cultures of Asia and Africa. *Google Book Search*. Web. 14 Oct. 2010.

4. "Freedom in the World—North Korea (2010)." *Freedom House*. Freedom House, 2010. Web. 14 Oct. 2010.

Chapter 5. Cults of Personality, Propaganda, and the Secret Police

1. Nikita S. Khrushchev. "The Secret Speech—On the Cult of Personality, 1956." *Modern History Sourcebook*. Paul Halsall, 1998. Web. 14. Oct. 2010.

2. Natan Sharansky. "The Prescience of Protest." *Los Angeles Times*. Los Angeles Times, 26 June 2009. Web. 14 Oct. 2010.

3. Jeffrey Brooks. *Thank You, Comrade Stalin!* Princeton, NJ: Princeton UP, 2000. Print. 61.

4. "Arch of Neutrality." *Atlas Obscura*. Atlast Obscura, 2010. Web. 14 Oct. 2010.

5. Peloso, Jennifer, editor. *The Two Koreas.* New York: H.W. Wilson. 2004. Print. 35.

6. Ibid.

7. Park Hyun Min. "Idolization Ever Increasing." *DailyNK*. DailyNK, 5 Dec. 2008. Web. 14 Oct. 2010.

8. Adolph Hitler. *Mein Kampf.* Vol. 1, Ch. X. *Hitler Historical Museum*. Hitler Historical Museum, 2008. Web. 14 Oct. 2010.

9. United Press International. "North Korea Covered by Slogans." *Space War*. Space War, 3 Oct. 2005. Web. 14 Oct. 2010.

10. "Constitution of the Communist Party of China (Amended and Adopted at the 16th National Congress of the Communist Party of China on Nov. 14, 2002)." *Chinatoday.com*. InfoPacific Development Inc., 2010. Web. 14 Oct. 2010.

11. "The KGB's 1967 Annual Report." *Cold War International History Project Virtual Archive*. Woodrow Wilson International Center for Scholars, 2010. Web. 14 Oct. 2010.

Chapter 6. The Right to Vote

1. Bureau of Democracy, Human Rights, and Labor. "2009 Human Rights Report: Cuba." *US Department of State*. US Department of State, 11 March 2010. Web. 14 Oct. 2010.

2. "Background Note: Zimbabwe." *US Department of State*. US Department of State, 23 Apr. 2010. Web. 14 Oct. 2010.

3. Chris McGreal. "'Vote Mugabe or You Die.' Inside Zimbabwe, the Backlash Begins." *guardian.co.uk*. Guardian News and Media Limited, 10 Apr. 2010. Web. 14 Oct. 2010.

4. "Background Note: Zimbabwe." *US Department of State*. US Department of State, 23 Apr. 2010. Web. 14 Oct. 2010.

5. Ibid.

6. "Background Note: Burma." *US Department of State*. US Department of State, 28 July 2010. Web. 14 Oct. 2010.

7. "Burma's Leaders Annul Suu Kyi's 1990 Poll Win." *BBC News*. BBC, 11 Mar. 2010. Web. 14 Oct. 2010.

8. Ibid.

Chapter 7. Human Rights

1. "Map of Press Freedom: 2010 Edition." *Freedom House*. Freedom House, 2009. Web. 15 Oct. 2010.

2. Carolyn Wakeman and San San Tin. *No Time for Dreams*. New York: Rowman, 2009. Print. 83.

3. Bureau of Democracy, Human Rights, and Labor. "2009 Human Rights Report: Cuba." *US Department of State*. US Department of State, 11 March 2010. Web. 14 Oct. 2010.

4. "Background Note: Cuba." *US Department of State*. US Department of State, 25 Mar. 2010. Web. 14 Oct. 2010.

5. Bureau of Democracy, Human Rights, and Labor. "2009 Human Rights Report: Cuba." *US Department of State*. US Department of State, 11 March 2010. Web. 14 Oct. 2010.

6. "Burma's Forgotten Prisoners." *Human Rights Watch*. Human Rights Watch, 16 Sept. 2009. Web. 14 Oct. 2010.

Chapter 8. Religious Practice and Culture

1. Karl Marx. *Marx on Religion*. Ed. John C. Raines. Philadelphia: Temple University Press, 2002. *Google Book Search*. Web. 14 Oct. 2010.

2. Mao Tse-tung. *Quotations from Mao Tse-tung*. "Chapter 32: Culture and Art." Beijing: Peking Foreign Language Press, 1966. *Mao Tse-tung Internet Archive*. Marxists.org, 2000. Web. 14 Oct. 2010.

Chapter 9. Totalitarianism and the Economy

1. Bill Powell. "The Next Great North Korean Famine." *Time*. Time Inc., 6 May 2008. Web. 14 Oct. 2010.

2. "2010 Index of Economic Freedom: Ranking the Countries." *The Heritage Foundation and the Wall Street Journal*. Heritage Foundation, 2010. Web. 14 Oct. 2010.

3. "Even with Access, Distributing Aid in Burma Is Difficult." *Daw Aung San Suu Kyi's Pages*. Daw Aung San Suu Kyi's pages, 30 May 2008. Web. 14 Oct. 2010.

4. Carolyn Wakeman and San San Tin. *No Time for Dreams*. New York: Rowman, 2009. Print. 115.

5. "The World Factbook: Burma." *Central Intelligence Agency*. Central Intelligence Agency, 29 Sept. 2010. 14 Oct. 2010.

Chapter 10. Daily Life

1. Dorothy and Thomas Hoobler. *The Cuban American Family Album*. New York: Oxford UP, 1996. Print. 20.

2. "Ten Principles for the Establishment of the One-Ideology System." *DailyNK*. DailyNK, 10 Oct. 2008. Web. 14 Oct. 2010.

3. Yoo Gwan Hee. "Modern North Korea Phones in Self-Criticism." *DailyNK*. DailyNK, 10 July 2010. Web. 14 Oct. 2010.

4. "The World Factbook: Burma." *Central Intelligence Agency*. Central Intelligence Agency, 29 Sept. 2010. Web. 14 Oct. 2010.

5. "The World Factbook: China." *Central Intelligence Agency*. Central Intelligence Agency, 29 Sept. 2010. Web. 14 Oct. 2010.

Chapter 11. International Relations

1. "The World Factbook: North Korea." *Central Intelligence Agency*. Central Intelligence Agency, 29 Sept. 2010. Web. 14 Oct. 2010.

2. "The World Factbook: China." *Central Intelligence Agency.* Central Intelligence Agency, 29 Sept. 2010. Web. 14 Oct. 2010.

3. "Nuclear Non-Proliferation Treaty." *US Department of State.* US Department of State, n.d. Web. 14 Oct. 2010.

4. "Burma's 1988 Protests." *BBC News.* BBC, 25 Sept. 2007. Web. 14 Oct. 2010.

5. "The Universal Declaration of Human Rights." *The United Nations.* The United Nations, 10 Dec. 1948. Web. 14 Oct. 2010.

Chapter 12. The Many Faces of Totalitarianism

1. Anthony C. LoBaido. "Harry Wu on the Real China: WND Interviews Former Political Prisoner, Human-Rights Champion." *WorldNetDaily.* WorldNetDaily.com, 5 April 2001. Web. 14 Oct. 2010.

2. "The World Factbook: Zimbabwe." *Central Intelligence Agency.* Central Intelligence Agency, 29 Sept. 2010. Web. 14 Oct. 2010.

3. "The World Factbook: Burma." *Central Intelligence Agency.* Central Intelligence Agency, 29 Sept. 2010. Web. 14 Oct. 2010.

4. "The World Factbook: Turkmenistan." *Central Intelligence Agency.* Central Intelligence Agency, 29 Sept. 2010. Web. 14 Oct. 2010.

5. "The World Factbook: China." *Central Intelligence Agency.* Central Intelligence Agency, 29 Sept. 2010. Web. 14 Oct. 2010.

6. "List of Electoral Democracies." *World Forum on Democracy.* World Forum on Democracy, 2000. Web. 14 Oct. 2010.

7. Gustaaf Houtman. *Mental Culture in Burmese Crisis Politics: Aung San Suu Kyi and the National League for Democracy.* Tokyo: Institute for the Study of Languages and Cultures of Asia and Africa. *Google Book Search.* Web. 14 Oct. 2010.

Index